50 Shades of Truth

Nikole A. Thompson

ISBN: 978-0-578-69036-0

Dedication

I would like to dedicate *50 Shades of Truth* to my husband, Anthony.

When all hope seemed lost, you never stopped fighting for the restoration of our marriage! You have always been my biggest supporter and encourager. Thank you for living your faith out in front of all of us so passionately. I am forever grateful that you came back to get me. Words can only capture a glimpse of my love for you. So, here's to the rest of our lives in love and ministry.

Contents

Acknowledgments

First and foremost, to our Heavenly Father, God. Thank you so much for sending your Son Jesus to resuce me from the destruction that became my life. The calling you have placed on my life I do not take lightly, and I live for the day when I can hear you say, "well done my good and faithful servant."

I wish to acknowledge each of the people listed below for what they mean to me:

To Anthony: My real life Hosea, the love of my life. Thank you for never giving up on us. Your example of Christ enabled me to become who God has called me to be.

To David B.: My daddy. Thank you for your selfless example of what a wise, loving father looks like and for embracing God's command to "train up a child in the way they should go." No matter how far I strayed, I could always rely on the love of God that lives in you to gently call me back home. Your intentional parenting has gven me the strongest foumdation, and I pray your legacy lives on through me, my children, and my children's children. To God be the glory.

To Jane Doe: I have sat in awe as I watched you blossom into a beautiful young woman, despite a season of tragedy. You are a walking, breathing, living, glowing testimony for the love of Jesus

Christ. If ever there was living proof of beauty for ashes… you sweet girl, are it. May God guide you, and may you live out your calling as He has destined you to live it.

To Kelly, James, Lindsay, Anthony, Michael, Matt, Alexander, Joshua, and Freddie. You each hold a very special place in this mamma's heart, and my prayer will always be for you to live out your God-given purpose. Also that you would be 10 times the parents your dad and I ever were. Be intentional!

To Alexander. Your Mother's Day/Birthday Present for 2020 was truly exceptional. You believed in me enough to invest in my time needed to isolate and focus on this book. Thank you for taking my dream seriously. That week in NOLA, my book took the actual shape God intended.

To Peggy and Roger: Your friendship is a gift. Your hospitality and kindness have never gone unnoticed. Your help with shaping this book early on through your insight and wisdom is appreciated more than words can express.

To Penny and Raymond: Thank you for listening to God and opening your home to us at the start of our ministry. God used that time to birth this book. You have always stood in the gap for me as an encourager, just as you do for so many others. Thank you for that.

To my spiritual mentors and mammas who collaborated with me and/or agreed to be first-time readers: Malia J, Chery S, Sherry H, Barbara D, Shonda G, Carol N, Tiffany H, Rachelle B, Lanay B. Thank you for your feedback and insight on a very hard topic. Your encouragement has kept me going when I wanted to give up. Your truths have kept me grounded and focused to write a book that is very relevant for our time, yet pleasing to God. Thank you for your input and guidance.

To My Front Row (naming just a few): To my sister, Shelly; my nieces, Lauri Ann and Kara; cousin and childhood best friend, Angel; and my sponsor Nicole. You each have walked very closely with me on this journey. Believing in this book for me when I didn't or couldn't. Your friendships have challenged me to not give up, and fight the good fight. Thank you all for pushing me to press on.

Pastor Elizabeth: Your impact in my life, the lives of my children and especially my marriage, was instrumental. The proof of your walk with Christ was so evident, when after eight years, you reached out through social media and embraced me once again. It was with your insight and wisdom that enabled me to find closure in the writing of this story.

To Jennifer H: You have truly helped me bring this book to life. You challenged me to dig deeply and share raw and vulnerable truths that would have otherwise never made it into the pages of this book. Your time invested alongside me in 2020, offering to partner with me, chapter by chapter, until *50 Shades of Truth* became a reality, is appreciated more than you could ever know! I am forever grateful for your friendship and all your expertise.

To my Covenant Church Family: Anthony and I have loved leading Celebrate Recovery for you, and do not take lightly the ministry you have entrusted to us. Your support and encouragement mean so much to us. It was your commitment that laid the foundation of strong biblical families and discipleship that has kept me focused on the need to get this message out there. God has used both Pastor Michael and Pastor Andrew, as well as others to speak directly to me many times over the past four years that I have been working on this book. I thank God for a church family who values the Word of God, and the call to be His hands and feet extended.

To Nellie K: Thank you for agreeing to be my editor. Your kind words the first time we spoke on the phone gave me such peace about working with you. You have brought wisdom to the table, and I am especially thankful for your partnering with me to get my words to print.

To Lonna G: I am amazed at how in just a matter of days, you took these pages and, from them, created this book. Layout and design does not nearly begin to describe what you have done in each and every chapter. This Christmas, I found great joy and excitement when I opened your email to see that you had created something so precious out of all my randomness.

To D.J. and Haylee: Thank you for bringing finality to this project. Everything from the vision for my cover, to the website design, to capturing the meaning behind each graphic design God had given me. Your talent and insight was able to capture and bring to life all of the random thoughts that I handed you. That is a special gift from God that will set you apart from others.

Introduction

Due to the strategic attack by Satan, I must warn you of the graphic nature of this book. It describes intimate details of my fall into sexual dysfunction, drug use, and rebellious living. More important, it is my story of deliverance. It is not my intention to offend; however, there are forces of good and evil each day which play a role in the many decisions all of us make. Being aware that this is a hot topic, our current culture pushes an "anything goes" mentality. I tread carefully. I do not want to be seen as glorifying my sin. I must remain vigilant that these topics could trigger someone. I simply want to make people aware of sexual chaos happening in front of our eyes. There will be Christians who find this offensive, and those from the LGBTQ community who will disagree with me as well. The Bible says, **"Darkness does not like light"** (see John 3:20). My goal is to shed light on this area that affects everyone.

It is our job as parents, grandparents, aunts, uncles, schoolteachers, and church members to understand and recognize what "this world" is coming to and not be afraid of it. We are the **"called out ones, a peculiar people"** (see 1 Peter 2:9). Strategically speaking, it is only wise to understand the plans of the evil one. We must understand that

"Satan comes to steal, kill, and destroy" (see John 10:10). So what is it about us that the Enemy wants to destroy? Primarily, he wants to destroy our identity in Christ. Satan tries to distort everything God does. Everything he offers is counterfeit to God's plan. John 10:10 says, **"I (Christ) have come so that they may have life and have it in abundance"** (HCSB).

Culturevated is my coined word for the mix of what our current culture represents and what is being cultivated within one's spirit. According to Webster's Dictionary,

- *Culture* is: 1. a: the customary beliefs, social forms, and material traits of a racial, religious, or social group. Also: the characteristic features of everyday existence (such as diversions or a way of life) shared by people in a place or time. b: the set of shared attitudes, values, goals, and practices that characterizes an institution or organization. c: the set of values, conventions, or social practices associated with a particular field, activity, or societal characteristic. d: the integrated pattern of human knowledge, belief, and behavior that depends upon the capacity for learning and transmitting knowledge to succeeding generations.
- *Cultivate* is: 1: to prepare or prepare and use for the raising of crops. Also: to loosen or break up the soil about (growing plants). 2: to foster the growth of. 3: to seek the society of: make friends with.[1]

---

[1] Merriam-Webster's Online Dictionary. Accessed October 17, 2020. *http://www.m-w.com/dictionary.*

The mix of these two words is what took place in my mind because of my surroundings: my people, places, and things. Due to the current culture (the world as a majority and its tolerance of homosexuality), and how cultivating—the laying of the groundwork, grooming, indoctrination, both in society and inside my home) were both lining up with homosexuality as the "acceptable and natural" way our world was progressing, I wrongfully took on this false narrative.

As I began this journey of putting my thoughts together for this book, I researched facts to present what God had revealed to me. I realized that our current culture had cultivated something inside me, something that 50 years ago may have never even been a thought, let alone an action. In this book, we will talk about hard topics that no one wants to discuss.

"God created us in His image" (see Genesis 1:27). God created marriage, and God created sex: **"And the two will become one flesh"** (Mark 10:8 HCSB). Why then have things become so out of control? Perhaps it started in homes where a parent or family member was a victim of sexual sin/misconduct; or perhaps it started in homes where honoring God is not the priority. Know one thing for sure, sexual sin has increased to become "an out of control" problem throughout society. The desensitization of our youth and adults happens frequently through our media and Internet. The Internet grants access to T.V., streaming, music apps, social media (Facebook, Snap Chat, TicTok, and Instagram), video games, and countless other apps available to our children 24 hours a day. It continues to grow, because Christians are either too fearful to approach the subject (and so we say nothing), or we are at the other end of the spectrum screaming; therefore, no one listens. James 2:13 says, **"For judgment is without mercy to one who has shown no mercy. Mercy triumphs over judgment"** (ESV). There must be a place in the middle where we address this situation with love and mercy, but still calling sin, sin. God's Word teaches us that all wrongdoing is sin. Without standing against these sexual perversions, the Enemy will continue to use the mainstream media to push his agenda. Thinking such as, *"Sex before marriage doesn't hurt anyone, swipe right and hook up with a one-night stand, it's all good; bisexuality is normal, everyone should do what just feels good, besides it's all just the same end result right? And doesn't God want me to be happy?"* On and on the lies go. With very few knowledgable enough or courageous enough to willingly stand up and speak out in love, these unhealthy patterns of sexual dysfunction continue to grow.

Due to my intimate understanding of thoughts that pave the way to a lifestyle choice of homosexuality, it is my sincere desire to shed light on an area where the Enemy has been running freely unchecked. Sexual sin is a serious issue in our culture and as Christians we are called to be **"wise as serpents and innocent as doves"** (Mathew 10:16 ESV). We are living in a generation where everyone can have an opinion EXCEPT Christians. I will be sharing the lies the Enemy plants within our children which contribute to this sexually explicit world.

By knowing the ways Satan is using the media (Internet) to influence our children and loved ones... (maybe even ourselves) toward sexual impurity, we can look for them, work to avoid them, and when encountered, stand against them.

This book is based on my real-life experiences, who I was in the past, and who I am today. God has written a beautiful story of restoration in my life. Looking back, I can see the process the Enemy used to *culturevate* a life of bisexuality within me. I would never have guessed that in the midst of my darkest days as I walked through the emptiest season of my life, numbing the pain with sex and drugs until enough was enough, God was still with me. Then He would **"give [me] beauty for ashes"** (Isaiah 61:3 NKJV). Through the restoration of my marriage upon my husband's release from prison, as well as the relocation of our little family, God was able to create in me the woman He had destined me to be. Reliving my past in order to get these truths out there has been painful. The process of owning the choices I had made and remembering just how far backwards the Enemy took me in such a short amount of time should be a red flag to everyone everywhere that Satan is committed to our destruction. Therefore, we must wake up. I know God's will for my life is to share my story. I want to expose the Enemy and reveal just how he planted these lies and half-truths deeply within me and kept me in bondage. The Enemy blinds us to God's truth and fills us with lies of unbelief that we have no value or purpose. Satan tells us we are too bad, too dirty, we have done too much—much more than anyone else—and we are too unworthy to come back to God. In fact, Satan wants us to believe we are too unworthy for God to love us. The absolute truth is: God loves us exactly where He finds us, but He loves us too much to leave us that way. Romans 5:8 says, **"But God demonstrates His own love toward us in that while we were still sinners, Christ died for us"** (NKJV). God's love is full of grace. He meets us right where we are at our lowest point, or what we think is our highest moment of pride itself. Yet, He does not want to leave us in the pit of sin, doomed to hell. There is no low where His grace won't go; there is no high where His grace can't find us.

Oftentimes, when we get saved or start serving God, we have a misconception that everything is going to be better automatically. However, we are responsible to **"renew our minds"** (see Romans 12:2). This means, in order to experience true freedom, we must be intentional about what we put into our minds and what we should avoid. In sharing my journey, my desire is that these examples of areas which have tripped me up, as well as the ways in which the Lord, His Word, other Christians, and life lessons have helped to create who I am today, can provide hope for your situation. No one is too far gone. God is no respecter of persons. Since He did it for me, He can and will do it for you!

I had gone two days without any sleep, two days with my mind racing, two days with all the natural tricks that lack of oxygen to the brain play on you, two days replaying his last words in my mind . . . "How does it feel to know how you're going to die?" That had been my ex-husband Tony's phone call to me earlier that month. That was the reason I didn't take the boys to the fall festival that year for John's birthday like every other year. I was afraid that Tony, this Tony, the enraged Tony, would harm me. I knew I had pushed him over the edge when he found and read my intimate letters to his friend. Sure, we had argued over the phone before and said many hurtful things. But it was the way he said this to me. Did he really want me dead? I had hung up immediately before giving him the time to elaborate. The fact that I signed the divorce papers on October 8 did not help the matter. I foolishly decided to stay awake, high on Methamphetamine . . . knowing that after days without sleep reality is no longer reality.

The kids were fast asleep. There was a knock at the door. Who could it be? My drug dealer had already left. Spaced out of my mind, I went to answer the door. Before I could even realize it was Tony, he was pushing his way through as I tried to shut the door. Anger was still written all over his face. My attempt to shut the door on him just sparked the fire of his rage even hotter.

We started arguing, and it did not take long for his anger to turn to pure mania. We spewed harsh words back and forth airing out each other's dirty laundry. It was as if we had forgotten that we loved each other so deeply at one time. We each justified ourselves with who had done what. You did this first, and if you had only. . . . The blaming went on and on as if we were puppets being moved by the Enemy himself to put the final nail in the coffin of our dead relationship. After all, our marriage was over. We were divorced. But to seal the deal, it was as if something supernaturally was moving us like pawns in a chess match, controlling each move we made. Each vicious outburst would cause deeper stings. It seemed the devil himself wanted us to grow deeper in our animosity and bitterness so that forgiveness would never be an option.

Unfortunately, Methamphetamine gives you a "false sense" of boldness that makes you think you are invincible. My words cut Tony like a knife. There had been many nights where I had allowed unchecked thoughts to race through my mind about all the mean and nasty things I would say to him. This seemed to be the perfect opportunity. Not until I found myself lying on the floor with a gun pointed at my head did I realize that maybe running my mouth was not the best option. When Tony's gun came out, I froze, silent, in total shock. His last words to me on the phone began to replay, "How's it feel to know how you're going to die?"

Would this be how I would die? Strung out! Drugs left out for my family to find! Which of my babies would wake to find their mother dead on the living room floor? My mind raced with panic and the worst of outcomes.

In the four years of our relationship, Tony had NEVER been violent. We had had a few arguments. However, he would always leave to defuse the situation. I had been told he had a temper . . . but honestly, I had never really seen it. With a gun to my head and tears rolling down my checks, I just lay there. I was too scared to scream and too frightened to fight. I had three babies in the other room. Tony was much stronger than I was, and I was too terrified to speak up anymore because it was obvious my words were only making things worse.

I cannot tell you what else he said. I cannot tell you when he left. It is just not in my memory. Maybe I tuned out what was happening. The night leading up to this incident and the rape itself replayed for years to come as a seed planted by Satan to inspire fear, hatred, bitterness, and resentment. Most of all, it fueled the excuse for me to continue blaming Tony and getting high. This scene would eventually be one of the seeds that birthed my bisexuality as Satan would whisper . . . "a woman will never hurt you like that; a woman could never overpower you like that; a woman would know how to treat you." Those would be the lies that Satan would replay in my mind.

Of course things did not start out like this. When we first met, honestly, I was so wounded, I had no interest in a relationship with anyone. But there was just something about him. He truly was one of the good guys. Tony did not smoke or drink, and he definitely did not do drugs. More important, he had full custody of his kids. What man in 1998 (more than 20 years ago) is raising five kids by himself? Tony reminded me of my dad. My dad has always been a huge hero in my life! To understand why I fell in love with Tony, you have to understand how I was brought up.

I originally wanted to write this book in third person. Ashamed of what some might think of me, I had to pray and seek God's direction for being this open and honest about my past. In looking back, I have been asking myself, *How did I get to that place?* Please know my heart. I never want to trigger anyone with my openness, and I know these are hard topics. I am not proud of the things I have done, but I am proud of what God was able to do in response to my desperate plea for help. When I submitted my life that was clearly falling apart in every way possible, God—and only God—could fix things. This book is the true story of my life, showing how quickly a marriage can fall apart and how, within the blink of an eye, drugs and sex can take over a person's identity.

This book also shares the process of how God cleaned me up. Within my story, I point out areas where the Enemy has access to influence our children. My prayer is that this, along with my real-life experiences of sexual dysfunction, will help to motivate you to understand the importance of the biblical truth found in **"guarding your hearts,"** (see Proverbs 4:23). In this fallen world where technology leads the way in everything we do, sexual sin is becoming not just accepted, *but protected,* and being pushed on our children through media, the Internet, and the political correctness that quenches the voice of God.

Chapter 1

Childhood: The Shaping of My Worldview

I believe in fairytale happy endings. It is my heart's desire to see the good in all people. Having been sheltered from most of the evil of this world until my teenage years, my viewpoint was naturally optimistic. I had a fortunate childhood, despite my parents divorcing when I was two. From age four to fourteen, I was raised by my dad with an older sister. At the onset of my teenage years, my sister was out of the house. It was just me and my dad who was wonderful to me.

My Dad

My dad was a third-generation lumberyard owner. He worked hard through the week and was off on weekends. My sister and I were latchkey kids until he got home at five. In a small town of two thousand residents, it really was not a big deal to be home without a parent. People laugh when I tell them we had only country music radio stations. Even our cable station would not allow MTV or VH1. I led a sheltered life. I played sports, attended church, took piano and flute lessons, and was in 4H every year. Where church was concerned, we never missed a Sunday service. My dad was active and present in all my activities. He attended every concert, tennis match, and 4H fair. Even if I did not qualify, he would take me to the state fair. We volunteered when any group needed help working in the concession stands. We also helped to build and decorate floats for local parades. We were always active in community events.

To say that my dad was involved in my life is an understatement. He took pride in helping me become the best version of myself. He didn't just attend my games; he also practiced with me during the week. He even taught me to bat left-handed. I remember complaining and wanting to give up, but he continued to remind me that we were not quitters and how left-handedness would give me an advantage. Then during tennis season, I must have practiced against our brick house for an hour every day. I never remember his demanding it; he just expected it, and I simply obeyed his preference. My father was self-employed, and this allowed him to invest time in my daily routine. We ate dinner together every night. He asked about my day, and we would make popcorn and watch movies. Minnesota winters are cold, and we would mix a gallon ice-cream container of homemade hot chocolate at the first sign of cooler evenings. We enjoyed Sunday meals at my grandparents' house and big holiday meals at my aunt and uncle's house. I had the storybook upbringing despite not having a mother present and active in my life.

We were not well off by any means, but I never wanted for anything. Dad never got welfare or food stamps for which he probably would have qualified. When I was eleven, Dad explained to me that if I wanted to make extra purchases, I would need to get a paper route and pay for items myself. If I wanted a big purchase, he would consider going in half with me. When it came to work, Dad allowed no excuses for absence. I had one of the longest paper routes in my hometown, which was two miles long. During hunting season, for safety reasons, my father would drive me. The rest of the year, despite all types of weather, I set out on my bike to deliver papers seven days a week. I am so grateful for the work ethic my father instilled in me.

Dad taught me other valuable lessons as well. Church was a priority. I still remember the first time I wanted to skip Sunday church service; I might have been thirteen or fourteen. My dad told me how his father told him one day, "David, it doesn't matter what you do during the week. I don't care if you stay out all night on Saturday, but you give God Sunday." My dad lived that lesson out in front of me. There was never a Sunday that we missed church. Even on vacations, we found a Lutheran Church to attend. Proverbs says, **"Train up a child in the way he should go and when he is old, he will not depart from it"** (22:6). I know in my heart of hearts that this foundation is how I was able to walk away from the destructive lifestyle I lived later. For me, having a loving father made it easy to see God as a loving Father. After some terrible times later in life I was still able to return into the arms of my Abba Father.

Looking at my childhood, several things really stand out. Most people who end up addicted trace it back to trauma while growing up. Many are abused or molested, or see things that they should not have been exposed to. I do not really fall into any one of those categories. My father never brought a woman home. For the ten years we were living together, he would date; but he never brought a girlfriend into our home. He wanted to raise me and parent me well. He was intentional about not spending intimate time with women in front of me. Most other kids of single parents in our community had the opposite homelife that I had. My dad wanted to be a good parent, so he put his personal life on hold.

My heart aches when I think of the three and a half years I was in the drug world. I regret the years I did not uphold honorable standards in front of my own boys. However, God brought about my freedom at a later date. I worked hard to demonstrate marital purity as something I could still fight for and instill into our boys.

Leaving Home

At age fourteen, I decided I wanted to move away from home to be with my mom. This was a huge change going from the small town of Springfield, Minnesota, to Evansville, Indiana, where there were two hundred and fifty thousand people. Mom had never shown a strong presence in my upbringing. It seems that I went years without her calling or even writing. My dad would drive us 800 miles at Christmastime to her sister's house to visit with my mother's side of the family. Even now, I realize that longing for both parents even when you have the happiest of childhoods is just there. Regardless of how good I had it, that desire to be a daughter and to have both parents support me and the need to be loved eventually manifested in unhealthy ways. I did not know my identity as God's daughter. My choice to make the move to Mom's house was mixed with the onset of teenage rebellion, curiosity about my mother, and a desire to be around my older sister and her children.

What a drastic change. With minimal supervision and no neighbors who knew me or cared about me like at my dad's, I ran wild. During my freshman year in high school, I started smoking cigarettes, drinking, smoking pot, and having sex with the neighbor boy. Looking back, I see that I was allowed way too much freedom. My fourteen-year-old self was too irresponsible to handle the move. This has taught me that even the most responsible kids and teenagers do not have enough wisdom to make choices that are not filtered through a caring and wise parent.

My Mom

My mom was a hard-working and very intelligent woman. She loved the Lord but did not have much of a personal walk with Him. She went to church as we all did, but that was it. We had no Sunday school, Bible classes, Wednesday night church, or fellowship with other believers. We did not listen to Christian music or watch positive faith-filled movies. We attended only Sunday morning church. We were pew sitters. I know now that those kinds of Christians are often hollow and have Jesus as only part of their lives. Because of this, they often quickly break under pressure.

My junior year in high school was a huge turnaround for my life. I have always been above average in intelligence. I would get so bored in class! My mom decided to switch me to an alternative school just five blocks from our house. My mom had recently gotten divorced for the third time. (This divorce was harder on her than the others because her husband left her for her sister.) She became depressed. Looking back, I see how she tried to numb her pain with drinking, dancing, and karaoke. We both had always loved to sing. We found a local bar that had karaoke and didn't card me. My mom did not seem to have a problem allowing my young pretty face to get us free drinks most weekends. While under the influence of alcohol, I had a one-night stand. I ended up pregnant at sixteen. I did not know I was pregnant until six months later. This all took place at the end of January 1995.

First Baby

Around that same time, my mom, who was working for a nonprofit home for girls, had been injured in an altercation between two of the girls. She was seriously hurt and needed surgery. To make things worse, her job did not offer workman's compensation. This left us in a bind. We had to move into a one-bedroom house to save money. My little brother, Glen, then eleven, got the bedroom. Mama's hospital bed was set up in the dining room, and I slept in the living room. To help my mom pay bills that summer, I worked the third shift for forty hours a week at the local Denny's Restaurant. Mom had her back surgery, and at that same time, I found out I was six months pregnant. You may ask how I could not know? I was on the Depo-Provera shot. I was told that I would gain ten to twenty pounds and would not have a period. I never even suspected I was pregnant. Before finding out I was pregnant, I honestly thought the small flutters I felt in my abdomen were gas bubbles. After I found out about my pregnancy, it seemed quite obvious that I had a baby growing in my belly. So here we were in the super-hot months of July and August just wondering how we were going to make it. We wondered what we would do and where I would even put a baby crib, because we were already living on top of each other.

My mom has always been one of the most resourceful women I have ever known. From her hospital bed she began to write everyone. She wrote to the mayor, her state representative, congressmen . . . I mean everyone. Within sixty days, she got us approved for section eight subsidized housing (normally a 12-18-month process). We moved into a beautiful huge three-bedroom home where I had a mini apartment upstairs for me and my baby son. Looking back, I know my parents simply did the best they could.

I never considered having an abortion with this pregnancy. I simply believed that was wrong. I considered this a situation that I had gotten myself into. As a strong independent woman, I knew I could make it. Finding out at six months that I was pregnant, an ultrasound machine revealed my baby's heartbeat to me. I never considered John a lifeless blob of tissue. I knew he was a real baby.

I finished high school four months early and graduated from Bosse High School in 1996. I continued to work at Denny's where I met my next boyfriend, Jeff. As soon as I turned eighteen, I moved into Covert Village, a section-eight apartment, and started my first year of college at the University of Southern Indiana. In the fall just after my son, John's, first birthday, I went to the doctor to get on birth control. However, it was too late. I was pregnant again by my new boyfriend. I quickly regrouped and switched to IVY tech with a major in marketing in order to shorten my time in college.

Someone mentioned abortion to me with this pregnancy, but I had a great deal of family support to keep my baby. I knew in my heart that love is the number one thing and that everything else would just work out. My family of origin does not exactly look traditional. I have an older brother who is adopted—an African American. It did not bother me that my sons would have different last names, or even look different. To me, bringing them up in a home that loved them in an environment like I was brought up in was all that was important.

I switched jobs to work part time at a mortgage company as a telemarketer. It was not the easiest life, but I was a young mom doing the best I could. Jeff and I continued to date, but we damaged our relationship early on. I cheated on him before I got pregnant, and he cheated on me during my pregnancy and after I gave birth to our son, Miles.

I personally felt I had no self-worth and no positive identity. After Miles' first birthday, I found out about another girl at Jeff's work with whom he had cheated while we were together. Hearing that, I blew up and kicked him out. I was broken, lonely, and only twenty years old with two kids by two different dads. I decided to turn to alcohol. A friend let me use her information to get a fake ID. During the summer of '98, I was bar bound almost every night. I found myself doing what my mom always had done after her breakups—numb the pain with drinking.

Chapter 2

Being Good Is Simply Not Good Enough: Marriage the First Time

My niece was my babysitter, and my looks paid the tab at the bar like they did in my teens. I met a man named Tony one day while dropping the boys off at my sister's house before going out. Tony was best friends with my sister's boyfriend, Harley. Tony noticed me while I was taking my boys into the house. He immediately drove around the block in his car to come back and approach me. We talked about that first encounter many times. Tony says there was a light on the inside of me that drew him to me. It was the joy of the Lord or something! He sensed a sweet innocence he was not used to. He asked me to go out with him that night. I had ended my relationship with Jeff a few months back. Still heartbroken and not interested in a real relationship in any way, I told him I did not have a thing to wear. At that moment, I was in some hot pink super short shorts. He smiled and said, "Hop in, and I'll take you to buy an outfit." I realize now looking back twenty years later that no man had ever bought me a gift or new clothes. The only things any guy had ever bought for me were drinks in hopes of having sex with me. My sister and her boyfriend, Harley, assured me I would be safe shopping with Tony, and that he would do exactly what he said he would do by taking me to a store for clothes. I vaguely remember Harley saying what a good thing this was because Tony would buy our drinks all night long. I got in, and Tony did just what he said he would. We went to a department store, and he waited while I picked out three or four outfits that I liked. He said, "Now try them on, and we can pick the one we like." We chose an outfit, went back to Lynn and Harley's house to get ready, and met them at Third Base, a small local bar with karaoke. The first song Tony sang for me was "Gangster's Paradise," a rap song by Coolio.[1] I was pretty sure he picked this song because of my presumed age. At this time, I was only twenty. Tony was thirty-six with no idea I had a fake ID. Tony had been in recovery for two years from smoking cigarettes, drinking, and drugs. Even though he did not drink like the rest of us, he was so much fun. He was a high-energy guy and full of

---

[1] Coolio, "Gangsta's Paradise," From Music from the Motion Picture Soundtrack, Dangerous Minds (Universal City, CA: MCA Soundtracks, Â1995).

life. He got up on the stage and sang any song from country to rap to rock and roll, and his favorite—screaming metal.

Tony and I continued to date for two weeks before we had our first kiss. His understanding and willingness to go slowly, and just get to know me was refreshing. We went to the drive-in one time, karaoke another, and one Saturday we drove ninety miles to my mama's house. He put up a fence for her. My mom said then that he was a keeper. I knew Tony had custody of his kids, but I had not really met them yet. About two weeks into our relationship on a Saturday night, we went out to sing karaoke. My sister was watching Tony's kids. My boys were staying at their cousins' house. I was too drunk to drive home, so I spent the night.

That Sunday morning was the "aha" moment for me with Tony. Until then, he was just a man with a lot of great qualities. He was hard-working, kind, and capable of fixing things around the home. He was raising his four boys and a daughter in a drug and alcohol-free home. Really, he reminded me of my dad. On that Sunday morning, he lined up his four boys. He had a squirt bottle in one hand and a brush in the other. He would fix the first one's hair, tuck in his little shirt,

Daddy showed me that parenting is more than just providing, that oftentimes we must put our selfish wants and desires on hold for the good of the family as a whole.

wipe off any leftover breakfast from his face, and then move to the next one. It was a little assembly line that instantly captured my heart. Here was a dad, doing the best he could do on his own. This aha moment where I fell in love with Tony wasn't because of his looks, or his ability to talk smoothly; it was because I watched him interact with his kids. He was an amazing Dad, and I had two boys that needed a Dad. I knew they needed someone to show them what it looked like to be a man. It was my job as their mother to find the right kind of man to teach them these things.

One random afternoon close to the end of my breakup with Miles' dad, I had been outside playing with my two boys. When Jeff pulled up, he got out of the car and immediately said, "Where is daddy's boy?" He said this all the time, and I honestly never thought anything of it. Of course, Miles then just learning to walk waddled up to his daddy, lifted up his arms to be held, and they hugged and bonded. It was a beautiful moment until I looked over at John. He was 2 ½ years old just standing there with a look—a look like, "Who is excited to see me?" Or "Where is my daddy? What about me?" It was then I realized that even though Jeff loved his son, the decision to love someone else's son as your own is a hard action to carry out. Never having had a faithful relationship, and never seeing a happy or healthy marriage, I did not know things could be better.

In the early stages of our courtship, I found out that Tony's oldest son Allan was not even his. He had adopted Allan while he was still married to

his ex-wife. They had divorced just months before we met and started dating. When his ex-wife left him, she gave over full custody of all the kids to let Tony raise them. After getting these three kids from his ex-wife, an ex-girlfriend with whom he had two children also gave custody to Tony. He literally had custody of five of his six children with Allan being the oldest, not even biologically his. The thing that intrigued me was that you could not tell a difference of which one came from where. Tony just loved them all and loved them the same. He took in my two boys like it was nothing. I knew that was what I had always wanted to be able to provide for my kids—a mom and a dad who loved each other and them, training them up to become all they could be.

Falling in Love

I was all in. Now, do not think it was just about what I could get . . . I honestly believe that God sent me to Tony to help with his children as well. Not only did my boys need a father, a man who could teach them all the things I could not; but also, his children needed a mother. Our first Christmas together I found out they had never made their own stockings or Christmas cookies. I remember the first time they told me they had never had homemade rice crispy treats. My heart just ached. Growing up with my grandmother, baking and desserts along with Sunday meals after church were all normal. How could these kids have never made the easiest three-ingredient dessert ever—rice crispy treats?

I found no fault with any of our exes for how they had chosen to participate or not to participate in our story. One thing also has to be clear; I have forgiven my mom for areas where she just did not know any better. I believe that was the case with my husband's exes and my boys' fathers . . . maybe they were never taught what intentional parenting looks like. But my father showed me, so I could never say I did not know. For the good of the children, I was called to do more, and I knew better!

Along with being a loving father, Tony was also a man of exceptional integrity. I remember one time when the phone rang, I told him who it was. He said he did not want to talk to the person. I offered to answer and tell the person he was not there. No big deal, right? Tony stopped me from lying on the phone. He answered the call and told whoever was on the other line that he would talk to him later. Then when he hung up the phone, he told me, "We don't lie. If I do not want to talk, I'm man enough to tell the person myself." To me, this was a really big deal, because my dad did not lie either. I guess when you are around people who tell "little white lies," it becomes normal and you do not question it. To meet someone committed to telling the truth caught me off guard in a positive way.

Tony had always treated me better than I had ever been treated before. At Jonathon's third birthday party we were at "Tunnels of Fun"

Amusements. I remember being in flip-flops and that in order to climb in the tunnels with the boys I had to wear socks. I may have mentioned going to get some, then got distracted talking to friends and family. Moments later Tony came back from buying me a pair of socks. He knelt down, took off my flip-flops, and put the socks on my feet. I remember everyone being so moved at how thoughtful he was. Small acts of kindness that I had never experienced before drew me to Tony. We dated for a few months, then Tony wanted to get married. We were sleeping together. Even at that point in his life, Tony knew that being together before marriage was not God's best for us. We continued to date, with marriage being brought up a lot in conversation. I moved in with him in November, and we were married in the Henderson Courthouse on December 2, 1998.

Making a Home

We spent the first year of marriage blending our family. There were now six boys and one girl. We were packed into a three-bedroom shotgun house. It did not seem to matter because we were growing together. In the beginning of '99, Tony had back surgery. I still worked at the mortgage company. Tony was receiving workman's compensation from Toyota, and then he drew unemployment. We found out I was pregnant in the first part of 2000, so we knew we needed a bigger house. We found the perfect five-bedroom home just ten blocks from where we were living. It had a double lot and a two-car garage. We moved in the spring and rented our other house to a family member.

One of my first memories in this house was a phone call from Betty (Harley's mom). I must have been about seven or even eight months pregnant. I was just huge, doing my dishes, when the phone rang. It was Betty asking if Tony or I had seen Harley in the past two days. I told her no. Then she said she was worried about him. She had checked with my sister Lynn who had not seen him. She paused, then she said she had even checked with his mistress, who had not seen him either. Mistress! Did she just say mistress like it was no big deal? I was sick to my stomach. How dare she call me looking for her son who was cheating on my sister. I assured her I had not seen him and had to quickly get off that phone before I would tell her just what I thought about her son cheating on my sister. I hung up that phone, and I remember thinking to myself as I rubbed my huge belly, "The day Tony Thompson doesn't come home all night, well, that's the day we get a divorce." That was my proverbial "line in the sand." Now, remembering that conversation . . . remembering how I felt at that moment, I would have never believed that within just a year and a half I would be willing to compromise. You could never have convinced me that in time I would adjust that boundary and justify why it was no big deal for Tony to stay away days on end.

By summer, we were ready for the baby. Tony's back was completely healed, and he was ready to go into the workforce again. He signed up at the Union and took the first job they offered him. Unsure about leaving me alone so late in my pregnancy, he had a friend stay with me during the day.

Our Own Business

In July, a woman approached Tony about a construction job one night while he was playing pool. She knew of him and that he was handy. She inquired if he could do a roof job ASAP. This was the beginning of our owning our own company—Thompson's Construction, Inc. Tony knew all the handymen from back in his partying days. His heart was in the right place, desiring to help provide financial security for these old friends. However, looking back, he could see these old friends were the foothold the Enemy used to get into our home. We know firsthand the truth behind, **"bad company corrupts good morals"** (1 Corinthians 15:33 CSB). Where we once had never allowed smoking or drinking on our property, it was just a few short months into owning this business that it became an everyday occurrence. By the end of 2000, God had blessed us with a very profitable business. We employed up to twenty-four guys at any given time. We even hired guys who came to us out of the drug rehab house.

With the birth of Thompson's Construction, Inc. also came the birth of Steven. On August 13, I checked into the hospital to have my labor induced. As you can imagine, with seven other children, it was quite a feat to find secure babysitters for all of them while I scheduled Steven's birth. After twelve hours of trying to start my labor, the doctor told me we would need to try again in one week. One of my strongest qualities is that I am a planner. Not having Steven on this day was NOT part of MY plan. I asked for a C-section because I wanted to deliver the baby that day. The doctor assured me that I would have to come back the next week because a C-section is not allowed unless a person is so many weeks overdue, which I was not. I broke down fanatically, expressing how we had seven kids and did he know how hard it was to find child care and safe places for them to spend the night and get to school in the morning? He was not very sympathetic. In fact, he rudely asked me if I had set up a tubal ligation, so I would not have this "problem" again. I remember thinking seriously, *"Did he just ask me that?"*

Thankfully, setting up the kids' care was not as overwhelming as I had envisioned. We came back to the hospital the evening of August 20, and by mid-afternoon the next day, Steven was born. Throughout my whole pregnancy, Tony had been telling me that the one thing he was unwilling or unable to do was to hold a newborn. Although he had several other children and had been to the hospital after they were born, he had never held a newborn. He kept saying they were breakable and too fragile. Tony agreed to be in the delivery room with me which was amazing. With my other births, I never had the baby's father in the room, so having Tony there created a bond between us that I cannot quite explain. It remains one of the top ten moments in our marriage that solidifies my love for Tony. As he stayed near my bed through the birth and then showed up later at my side, he had a look on his face I had never seen—awe, wonder, and joy, an unspeakable joy beamed from his face as he carried our son to me. To know Tony is to know that most of the time what he says is final. I never dreamed he would swoop up our baby and so proudly carry him to me. On August 21, our family literally became "Yours, Mine, and Ours." God's perfect timing for Steven's birth prevailed in a wonderful way over my fears and need to control the circumstance.

Tony and I were drug and alcohol free for our first two years of marriage. It really was our desire to help people. But with no foundation in God's Word to define right and wrong for us, our values were easily swayed. You have to know the answer you are going to give when temptation shows up at your door. Satan did not show up to my husband's doorstep with a bag of Meth and a beautiful nineteen-year-old woman. The deceiver showed up slowly, asking us and tempting us to compromise one step at a time. With no real biblical foundation, the good in our lives soon became corrupted by those we sought to help.

With no real biblical foundation, the good in our lives soon became corrupted by those we sought to help.

Beginning the Downward Turn

An "aha" moment for Tony came the day he looked back and could see how he opened the door for the Enemy to enter our home. It played out like this: It was the end of a normal day. Many of the workers would come get cash advances on the work they had done. One worker came to Tony with a different question. Jesse was our siding applicator who was about halfway done with his current job. We had at least two more houses on the back burner for him to complete. Jesse waited until everyone left and approached Tony asking if Tony could get him a bag of pot. Jesse said his normal guy was out, and he really wanted some. Tony's first response was a firm, "NO WAY, you know I don't mess with that stuff anymore." Jesse replied, "Yeah, but you still know people who do." This incident reminds me of the snake in the Garden asking Eve, **"Did God really say?"** (Genesis 3:1 CSB). Tony stuck to his "No," and the guy turned to leave. Conflicting thoughts flashed through my husband's mind, and in just seconds, the time it took for Jesse to get to the front door, this thought scene played out. Tony pictured this Jesse, a long-haired, hippie-looking guy who weighed about 150 pounds at 6 feet 2 inches tall, driving a beat-up truck with no brakes, no exhaust, no insurance, and a suspended license. The thought of Jesse on the hunt looking for a bag of weed and getting pulled over and put in jail tormented Tony. Who would finish this job? Jesse had already collected pay advances against his present work. Who knows how much the bond would be if Jesse got arrested? We had back-to-back jobs lined up. Just seconds after Tony's answer: "The answer is still no," he called to Jesse and said, "Wait, I'll call a guy." It is sad now looking back at our morals and standards, because even though we were not doing drugs or affiliated with drugs, we had a family member in our rental house. Tony knew he was selling weed. Tony made the call, asked to send Jesse over, and his response was, "Man, you haven't been out of the game that long that you forgot how this works. You ain't sending just anyone to my house. I know you. You come." Tony went. He got a bag of marijuana, brought it to Jesse, and said, "Now, when this is gone, that's it. No more." The next day another worker came to Tony wanting a quarter pound, and Tony stood to make $100.00 just to do the trade. We were bringing home thousands of dollars a week after paying our guys. We did not need the money. And yet within two weeks of that first sale, Tony was driving to Chicago every other week and unloading about twenty pounds per trip. I literally had an empty vacuum cleaner box in my bedroom that perfectly held all 20 bags as we got rid of them each week.

Once we had become accustomed to this side income, another worker approached Tony to tell him how the pot was only a little money compared to what we could make by producing and selling Meth. By our youngest son's first birthday, just a little over one year since that day when I stood in my kitchen and swore I would leave Tony Thompson the night he did not come home, Tony was staying away more nights than he spent at home. Infidelity had crept into our marriage, and I stood by and said nothing. I did not know about the cheating for a fact, but deep down I knew something was not right. I somewhat justified him being gone because he brought in good money. Meanwhile, I was the soccer mom driving all the kids to the YMCA for swim lessons and taking our daughter to gymnastics. I was constantly filling my time with the kids but had lost touch with Tony.

September 21, 2001, was the first time I went to jail. Tony and I were pulled over and arrested on our way to drop off some weed before going to a God Smack concert. We were questioned and then taken to spend the night at the Evansville County Jail. Looking back now, I can see that my husband had a cocky streak. The day we got out of jail he bought a 2001 GT Mustang. I remember he told me it was so the cops would not recognize him in a new car.

Shortly after our arrest, several people, including my family members, came to tell me Tony was cheating on me. Again, I believe I knew it all along, but I just did not want to admit it. He continued to cheat and stay away many nights. I did not want to leave the marriage, but it got to the place where I did not even recognize who I was anymore. My hopes of a marriage where Mom and Dad took the kids camping or to the movies on the weekend seemed to be fading away. Tony and I did so many things with the kids the first two years of our marriage; but the construction company gave both of us a second life. I was not pushing for Tony to be home and eat dinner around the table like we had the first two years. I would make excuses to the kids as to why he was gone and would shower them with gifts or take them places. I honestly wanted a Christian marriage, but I had just never seen one to know they existed or how to help us have one.

As I became aware of Tony's infidelity, I began to evaluate what our marriage had become. I was staying home taking care of the kids while he did whatever with whomever he wanted. I began to want to leave. But how? Thompson Construction existed because he knew the workers. Tony had a large contract with a company in Indianapolis. Sure, I owned 49 percent, but what good was that on a monthly basis? How would I even provide for myself? So, by the end of 2001 or the beginning of 2002, I started looking for a job with the intention of leaving Tony when I was able to provide for myself and my three biological sons.

At the end of January 2002, Tony was arrested again with his nineteen-year-old girlfriend, Sarah. This time his bond was set for $5,000 cash. He called me and cried. He said all the right things. He made promises to never stay away again. I still remember the jailer's face when I put the five rolls of $1,000 bills through the metal detector to go and bond him out. He looked down at all that money and asked me, "Is he worth it?" I was confident that he was. However, he quickly broke his promises, staying away that first night and many thereafter. All those smooth-talking promises made over the phone were broken and justified as soon as he was released.

Remember in the beginning when I told you I was a fairytale person? I do really try to see the good in all people. My love for Tony somewhat blinded me. I had gotten to a place where I blamed the other women and not Tony. I wanted to retaliate against them as if the affairs were all their fault. A few times I found out where they were, and I showed up to fight. After all, the Bible does say in Numbers 32:23,

"Your sin will find you out" (NKJV). It is crazy looking back now at how God confirmed Tony was cheating in order to give me the strength to leave. In March or April of 2002, I had come home on my lunch break and left a card begging Tony for us to go back to the way things were, saying we did not need the money from drugs, begging him to please choose me. On my way to my car heading back to work, the neighbor from across the street called me over. Concerned that I was being naïve, she confirmed that not only was Tony cheating on me, he was bringing another young girl into our home while I was at work, bringing her around our kids. Before thinking, I called my job and made up a reason to miss that afternoon. I drove around the house and planned how to hide without their knowing I was in the house. I parked my car three blocks away in an alley and walked to our house. I went in the back door and then hid in my bedroom behind the door.

Thoughts flooded my mind. I got angrier and angrier. Sure enough, two of our kids came in after school and so did this young girl. I sat there at first paralyzed that the rumors were true. He was seeing her and bringing her into our home while I was at work. Heartbroken but angry, I came running out of the bedroom. I pulled her off the couch and trapped her hips between my knees. I double wrapped her long hair in my left hand and I just started hitting her, punching her with my right fist. Tony was outside and came running in to pull me off her. As he pulled, I just pulled harder on her hair. He finally got me off her. He then loaded her and the kids into the car. He kept telling me that they were just hanging out, that they really were not together. But this was the girl he was arrested with in January. In my heart, I knew he was involved with her. Tony drove off, and I just wept. I fell to my knees and cried. I hated what I had become. I had never been an angry or mean person. Honestly, I am really a kind and loving person. But this Nikki who plotted and planned; this Nikki who felt good in that fight; that was an evil Nikki. I did not want to be her.

This was not the only time I blew up at another woman. One-time Tony called me by accident—a total "pocket" dial. I could hear him talking to May, a close friend of the family with whom he was cheating on me. I kept the phone on speaker until Tony gave away their location, a local cell phone store. I drove to the parking lot of the store and proceeded to go straight psycho. I called May every name in the book. I threatened to bash in the side window of that pretty new Mustang. After all, it was half mine. Oh, Tony was so mad, and angry at me. He yelled and screamed that I was overreacting and making something out of nothing.

I was in anguish over the amount of lies that swarmed around Tony and almost everyone he associated with once Methamphetamine entered his world. I see now why people needed to lie to me. They had to protect their habit by not alienating their supplier. It is really easy to sit on your pedestal and say, "I would never lie like that and cover up and make excuses for someone" when you are not in the drug world. But when you are addicted and just concerned about getting your next fix, you find yourself making many compromises. Now, I see the justifications in many I work with who are deceived by the Evil One, by darkness. When you are deceived, you just do not know until someone brings light and truth to that area. My heart wants to be culturally relevant without it becoming spiritually irrelevant. I continually have to check and recheck my motives with each statement to retain a God-centered worldview and not push my emotions on this topic.

Leaving Tony

I was so ready to leave Tony, but I did not know how I could get out with all our things. After all, he did not have a work schedule to follow. God knew I wanted out and did not know how to go about it. I felt so distraught. All my emotions were boiling over: anger, justification, sadness, rage, hopelessness. I was on a rollercoaster and wanted off. I called my dad and asked to borrow money to move out. I owned a car that was paid in full. I had been on my own before, and I thought it had to be better than this. Friends offered to help me pack up our belongings in the middle of the night. We planned to get a U-Haul and storage unit at daybreak. We would have everything safely locked up by 9:00 a.m., long before Tony would ever come home. That was the plan. I found a house. It just so happened to be the house where one of his girlfriends used to live. I rented the storage unit and planned to pick up the U-Haul at 8:00 a.m. Just like we planned, my items were all out of the house before Tony got home. When he arrived he was enraged.

I was settled in my next house by May 2002, and I was strong for a week. But Matthew 24:41 tells us, **"Watch and pray so that you will not fall into temptation. For the spirit is willing, but the flesh is weak"** (NIV). I honestly remember thinking about that song, "Housewife." It has a line in it that says, "You Can't Turn a Hoe Into a Housewife,"[1] and how my husband did not want a housewife. He wanted the hoe—a dirty fun sexual girl, not the boring housewife I had become. Satan painted to me a picture that had such a distorted truth to it. Oh, how I wanted him back. I missed him deeply. I started having these thoughts excusing him because I missed what we once had. Friends had confirmed that he was doing Methamphetamine now, so I called him. I invited him over and told him I wanted to get high with him.

I do not remember his hesitating. I remember how badly I was hooked both on Tony and the Meth. From June until October, I lived in chaos beside Tony. Many times, he would come by and get me a high, so I would be up all night. But he would never come back to stay. He was living a double life. I get it now, but then it only led to my reaching out for Meth to his partner who cooked it also. He was a much older married man. I knew he was interested in me, but he was one of the largest

[1] Dr. Dre, "Housewife," Hittman and Kurupt Album, 2001, Released in 1999.

dealers in town. I hung out for almost six months before finally sleeping with him for the drugs. I would imagine, looking back, he must have given me two eight-balls of fresh uncut Meth a week. I hated myself for sleeping with him, but I could never have afforded the habit otherwise. When addiction has you, you do things—things you would never even consider when sober. He was my hook-up for two solid years. I never wanted for Meth those two years. I had it every day. I believed I was a functioning addict because I maintained my job in corporate America, working 8-5 Monday through Friday.

During this season, I could not see any of my own compromises. My behaviors seemed to transition downward without my noticing. Think about some of these statements:

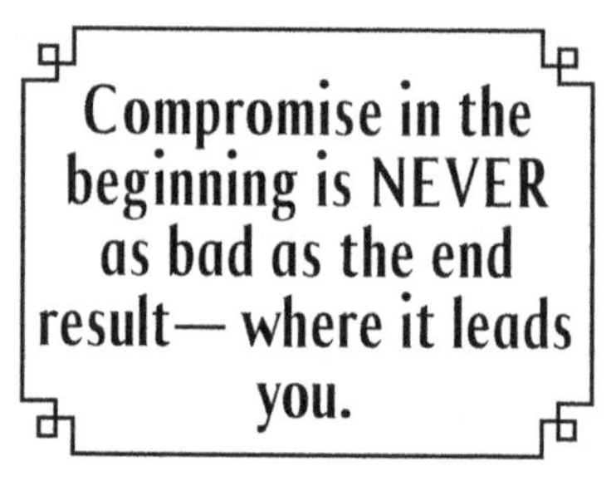

- I would never steal for my habit.
- I would never steal from my family for my habit.
- I would never steal from my children for my habit.
- Drinking is legal, I would never do illegal drugs.
- These pills are prescribed; I am not doing anything illegal.
- I would never try hard drugs like Meth or Heroin.
- I would never use the needle.

- I would never drink or do drugs while my kids were home.
- I would never drink or do drugs while my kids were awake.
- I would never drive my kids drunk or high (just myself).
- I would never tolerate my husband staying away all night.
- As long as he is here more than away, it is ok.
- I would never look the other way to an affair.
- I would never sleep with someone for drugs.
- I would never sleep with a married person for drugs.
- I would never let someone sleep with one of my children for drugs.

Take a moment, listen to the song "Slow Fade," by Casting Crowns. "Sin always gradually gets darker left unchecked."

After that younger girl came in and slept with my husband, I swore I would never do anything like that myself. When I said it, I really meant it. However, in addiction, you always do things you regret—things you wish you would not have done. Less than a year down the road, I became the very thing I hated and swore I would never become: A homewrecker who slept with the dope man just to get the dope. I would then lie about it because of how ashamed it made me feel.

Divorce

Tony continued to swoop in and swoop out of my life over the summer. He filed for divorce, and

I did not show up. Then I filed for divorce, and he did not show up. On October 8, 2002, we were officially divorced after several court appearances on my part. Midsummer, a warrant was issued for Tony in Indiana which explained why he would not show up in court. He had to be sneaky, he told me later, as he drove back and forth from Chicago to Evansville. He would stay in Illinois and cut over to Kentucky, then come from Henderson to Evansville. You never really know what is going on in the midst of active addiction, but with Meth, you think you know. You make up many stories in your mind. Your stories have stories, and soon it is hard to remember truth from lies, fact from fiction. I later found out that he was staying in a hotel in Henderson with a girl named Sarah. I am not sure how he or I ever imagined things were going to get better.

Angry at all the lies and experiencing a life of partying really for the first time in years, I justified talking to one of my husband's main friends behind his back. This friend had at one time claimed he was sleeping with Sarah in a letter he wrote me while he was in jail. I just liked the attention. We became pen pals. It is odd how quickly that sin nature of sexual immorality slips in. Fairly quickly, our letters took a turn toward the erotic. One random night when I was out, Tony came to my house. My niece was babysitting and did not see any reason to not let Tony in to see the boys. He began going through my things and found and read one of the letters. All I can say is, at the moment something snapped inside Tony. He often says that the day he was arrested, he was coming to deal out vigilante justice to anyone who had helped me get high, especially his "Meth partner," the older married man. He and I were not even sleeping together until after Christmas, but you could not expect Tony to believe that. Tony now thanks God often for God's mercy in having him arrested.

Tony's rage was founded on a double standard because Tony had multiple girlfriends. I, on the other hand, was supposed to remain faithful to him. In my newfound world of Meth addiction, I became extremely out of control almost immediately. Again, after Tony had heard I was flirting, approaching, and being with not just other men but his friends, he lost it.

The beginning of October just a few days after finding that letter, Tony called me and threatened me. In four years of being together with many ups and downs, Tony had NEVER been violent with me. I don't think it ever crossed my mind that our relationship would come to that point. The only reason I even remember this call, or the time frame was because I was scared to leave my house all that week. It was the week of our town's fall festival and normally I would take the kids. But this year I stayed hidden, locked up in the house.

I could not tell anyone what was really going on in my life. I did not feel comfortable even reaching out to my mom or sister. No one ever just says, "Look, I am on Meth, and I like it, and I am sleeping around, and Tony is furious with me." So instead, I just made Tony out to be the crazy one. He was on the run, and everyone knew it. He looked like he was on drugs, so that was not a far stretch of the imagination. Tony's personality had always been strong. He had a way of having the final say in almost everything. He made others around him somehow just submit to his ideas. He has always been a leader, and I knew from the beginning of our marriage that his say was always the final say. He was not mean about it, he just talked with authority. It was always his way or the highway.

I chose to continue to do Meth during these few weeks. (A drug that causes paranoia may have not been my best choice.) I had gone two full days without any sleep, two days with my mind racing, two days with all the natural tricks the brain plays due to lack of oxygen, two days replaying his last words in my mind . . . His most recent words to me had been," How does it feel to know how you're going to die?" I was afraid that Tony, this Tony, the enraged Tony, would harm me. I knew I had pushed him over the edge when he found and read my intimate letters to his friend. Sure, we had argued over the phone before and said many hurtful things. But it was the way he said it to me. Did he really want me dead? I had hung up immediately before giving him the time to elaborate. We were now officially divorced. So that did not help my situation. I foolishly decided to stay awake, high on Methamphetamine . . . knowing after days without sleep, reality is no longer reality.

A Night of Horror

The kids were fast asleep. There was a knock at the door. Who could it be? My drug dealer had already left. Spaced out of my mind, I went to answer the door. Before I could even realize it was Tony, he was pushing his way through as I tried to shut the door. It began with Tony demanding I make love to him. He told me if I really loved him, and if he was really the only one, I just needed to prove it. He said if the letters really meant nothing, if there was no one else for me, I would do what I was told. He could see I had put up a wall. Initially, I was too scared to even respond with words. Anger was still written all over his face. My attempt to shut the door on him had angered him more. The fact that I was not talking enraged him more. It was about this time I noticed the look in his eyes. Where love and compassion were once so clear, there was now just a cold dead stare. As he continued to bring up the disgusting letters he had found, quoting the vile things I had written, I felt something come over me. The shame and guilt turned to rage. The hypocrisy of it all! It was a total double standard! He would leave me for days on end. I knew he still had other girls, so I joined in the arguing. It did not take long for his anger to turn to pure rage. Meth gives you a false sense of boldness. We spewed harsh words back and forth airing out each other 's dirty laundry. It was as if we had forgotten that we loved each other deeply at one time. We each justified ourselves with who had done what. You did this first, and if you had only. . . . The blaming went on and on as if we were puppets being moved by the Enemy himself to put the final nail in the coffin of our dead relationship. After all, our marriage was over. We were divorced. But to seal the deal, it was as if something supernaturally was moving us like pawns in a chess match controlling each move we made. Each vicious outburst caused deeper wounds. We grew deeper in our hate and bitterness so that forgiveness would not be an option.

My words cut Tony like a knife. There had been many nights where I had allowed unchecked thoughts to go through my mind about all the mean and nasty things I would say to him, and this seemed to be the perfect opportunity to express myself. Not until I found myself lying on the floor with a gun pointed at my head did I realize that maybe running my mouth was not the best option. When Tony's gun came out, I froze, silent, in total shock. His last words to me on the phone began to replay, "How does it feel to know how you are going to die?"

In the four years of our relationship, Tony had NEVER been violent. We had a few arguments; however, he would always leave to defuse the situation. I had been told he had a temper . . . but honestly, I had never really seen it. With a gun to my head and tears rolling down my checks, I just lay there.

I was too scared to scream and too scared to fight. I had three babies in the other room. Tony was much stronger than I was, and I was too scared to speak up anymore, because it was obvious my words were only making things worse.

I cannot tell you what he said when he was done. I cannot tell you when he left because it is just not in my memory. Maybe I tuned out what was happening. The phone call, those words he said and the rape itself replayed for years to come as a seed planted by Satan himself to inspire fear, hatred, bitterness, and resentment. Most of all, it fueled the excuse for me to continue blaming Tony and getting high. This scene would eventually be one of the seeds that birthed my bisexuality as Satan would whisper . . . "A woman will never hurt you like that; a woman could never overpower you like that; a woman will know how to treat you." Those would be the lies that Satan would replay in my mind.

On October 17, Tony was picked up by the police in Illinois. Tony and Sarah, his girlfriend, were both placed in jail awaiting court. There were several charges this time, charges that he would not be able to deny. There were drugs, pills, and a weapon, not to mention he was also wanted in Indiana. There was no bonding out this time. The local cop who had been on the lookout for Tony was oh so happy to come and tell me of his arrest.

To understand the severity of a relapse, know this. Tony had been clean for more than five years before he picked up Methamphetamine, and within 120 days, he was locked up behind bars facing up to 96 years in prison. I will never tempt fate with that lie Satan tells everyone: "Just one more time." No Deal! My sobriety is a decision I make every single morning.

My Slippery Slope

Now of that last encounter with Tony, the Enemy did several things in my mind. He gave me ample reason to justify my drug use. Satan reminded me that I had tried to be a good wife, and this is what it got me. Why walk the straight and narrow? It did nothing for me. Memories of that night continued to be fuel for the fire of resentment in my heart. It served as a constant reminder of why I could never get emotionally close to another man. For the next three and a half years while Tony was behind bars, I spiraled out of control, getting high, drinking, and having sex with multiple people (always under the influence). I know Satan bombarded my mind with those thoughts to keep me feeling helpless and hopeless, to imprison me behind a life of drugs and alcohol. I realize now that I cannot blame Tony or that night for my decision to keep using drugs once he was locked up. I was simply addicted.

I enjoyed the edge these substances gave me at work in my sales position and how it allowed me to go to the club and dance and drink a few drinks without becoming so drunk that someone would take advantage of me. The Meth also helped me when I was too drunk and wanted to sober up. It helped me to lose weight, have energy to clean my house, and generally get more accomplished than anyone else. To the old Nikki, Meth seemed to keep me always in control, or so I thought. Looking back, I am so thankful that those three and a half years of drug use never left me in jail. You often hear stories of drug deals gone bad, reports of people losing their kids, or becoming a victim of sex trafficking. I thank God every day that I was never kidnapped and brutally raped by strangers. There are millions of ways my life could have been worse. People on drugs get in car wrecks all the time, and many die before their time. I am in awe of the hedge of protection that God placed around me in the midst of my unwise choices.

Chapter 3

Satan's Plans: Darkness, Destruction, and Death

First Corinthians 14:10 says, *"There are, it may be, so many kinds of voices in the world, and none of them is without signification"* (KJV). Every thought comes from somewhere. I will be sharing a great deal about the voices and thoughts—even thoughts I know Satan handed me and seeds he planted into my spirit. Bottom line—if it is not good, beneficial, and loving, it is not coming from God. And that means, it is coming from the other place, from your Enemy the devil who wants to destroy you. Bottom line.

When I was on my own in May 2002 (after packing up my belongings in the dead of night, and leaving in the U-Haul early in the morning before Tony would come home) I, all of a sudden, had this new freedom. I had never really been taught how to deal with my emotions. Yes, with my father, church was the go-to. However, moving away by age 14, I never really had any trauma for which I would need to learn healthy coping mechanisms. When I lived with my mother, her go-to during emotionally turbulent times was alcohol. That is what I instantly turned to as well.

It is crazy to think about all the mind games Satan used in order to toy with me. And it is not that I was some great wife for three and one-half years, because there are many things that I could have done differently to help my family! I could have gone to church with the kids, even if Tony didn't. I could have spoken my mind in love and confronted questionable things. I could have sought guidance from wise godly counsel. But instead, I did as the world does. I did what my mother had always done. I turned my back on Tony, our marriage covenant with God, and the kids. I found a way to separate and eventually divorce. I started over at 24. I knew that I could raise three boys by myself. I have always had a strong work ethic. I was confident that I could do this. After all, my mother had always demonstrated what a strong, independent woman looks like.

At age 24, separated, three kids by three different dads, what do you think my go-to was? Once again I began altering my state of mind with alcohol, numbing the pain. In the dark of night, the questions began to come. Why did he leave me? What wasn't good enough about me? Didn't I fulfill the role of a "good housewife"? Adding alcohol to my loneliness only complicated things more, because my love for Tony began to come back to life. Satan did not attempt to bother Jesus during His fast of 40 days until the very end when He was at a very weakened state. In a sober mindset, I was able to remember all the pain and all the hurt. But I believe the intoxicated state is when the thoughts of "You can't turn a hoe into a Housewife"[1] came into play. I began to long for Tony, for what we once had.

It was only one or two weeks of my being in my house "alone" before I reached out to Tony. And the introduction of Meth brought about a season of my life I once was so ashamed of, but now I remind myself: **"What the Enemy meant for harm God will use it for good"** (see Genesis 50:20). I remember this season, so I know I do not ever want to go back. I remember this season so I can tell others how God is a redeeming God. I remember this season not to ever glorify my sin, but to know God's forgiveness paid for all my sins. And, He wants me to tell others so they can walk in the freedom that I have found. **"He comforts us in all our affliction, so that we may be able to comfort those who are in any affliction, with the comfort with which we ourselves are comforted by God"** (2 Corinthians 1:4 ESV). It is this very reason we share out of the depths of our most painful seasons to give hope. He did it for me, and He will do it for you! God is no respecter of persons (Acts 10:34 KJV). **"Then Peter started speaking: "I now truly understand that God does not show favoritism"** (NET). Again, I never want to come across as glorifying my sin, and writing this book has been a long, painful process for me.

---

[1] Dr. Dre, "Housewife."

The summer of 2002 was all just a blur. I thought by sharing the experience of drug use with Tony I could win him back. This sounds so utterly ridiculous to me now. Honestly, it only served as fuel for me to become more angry and bitter. Satan would tell me in my mind I wasn't good enough to raise his kids; I didn't do a good enough job satisfying him; I wasn't skinny enough; I had gotten too old (I was 24 and a few of the girls with whom he had cheated on me were 18, 19, or 20). Just know when you think negatively and add drinking and Meth to it, you get lunacy.

Tony Arrested

By October 17, 2002, when Tony was arrested, I was in addiction, alcoholism, rebellion, and sexual dysfunction. I was spiraling out of control at an alarming rate.

While Tony was behind bars, he was looking for answers. After all, he had been sober two years when we married, five and a half years before his relapse. He wanted to know what happened, and he began a long journey with God. In the midst of his soul-searching and sitting at the feet of Jesus, I would receive letters from him four or five times a week. Each letter was filled with Scripture, how sorry he was, and how when he got out, we would do things differently. To me, it was jailhouse religion; and I laughed at these letters. I showed my friends these letters and mocked how he signed each and every letter, "Love always," and "Forever your husband, Anthony Thompson." We were not even married. Did he forget we were divorced? Little did I know God had told him to do that for the restoration of our marriage . . . that he needed **"[to call] those things which be not as though they were"** (Romans 4:17 KJV). Things did not look good for Tony on the inside. I rarely wrote to him; his friends (mostly Harley) wrote him confirming my sleeping around, my drug addiction, and how sick I looked physically because of the drastic weight loss. The first time I went to see Tony, the local jail chaplain met me at a fast-food place to discuss his opinion of Tony. It was not helpful. Now I see yet again the Enemy's hand in trying to end our relationship. This chaplain confirmed that indeed Tony was being truthful about studying the Bible; however; he also told me he had seen it happen many times. Jailhouse religion was very common, and whether this was the real deal or not, only time could tell. I just needed to hear there was a chance it was fake in order to justify not going to see him or trying to work on things. After all, I liked this new life of drugs and singleness, supporting myself with my job and doing what I wanted for a change. I only went to see Tony five or six times the whole time he was locked up. I cannot imagine the overwhelming weight that Tony felt under the conviction of the Holy Spirit, and Satan condemning him for my outcome. God taught Tony that he was the head of the house, the spiritual leader, and if he wanted to know where his family was, he only needed to look where he led us. I am amazed at the love that burned in Tony's heart for me. However, while he was locked up, I would not or could not give him the time of day.

Over the next two years, I would work in corporate America at OneStar and live this double life with an addiction to Meth.

I shared with you how I wanted to write this book in third person. Ashamed of what some might think of me, I had to pray and seek God for direction on being this open and honest about my past. Looking back asking myself how I got to this place, I was able to pinpoint a key song or video that stirred up something different inside. A stronghold was created. It was the year of my divorce, and I was spending a great deal of time in bars drinking, or high on Meth, just dancing the night away. A new techno song had hit the club, and I found myself singing the lyrics. But the tipping point was when I watched the video. It consisted of two teen girls, dressed in schoolgirl uniforms, making out in the rain.

In researching this song, I found the group producer who was very intentional about the creation of the group, as well as the creation of this video. When asked his purpose for pushing this song, paired with this video he stated: "I saw that most people look up pornography on the Internet, and of those, most are looking for underage sex. I saw their needs weren't fulfilled. Later, it turned out, I was right."[2] This is the same as my own desires. I prefer underage girls.

---

[2] Ivan Shapovalov, Website: IMVDB, author: Adam Fairhom (Oct. 6, 2020). *https://imvdb.com/blog/2014/02/music-video-relapse-all-the-things-she-said-by-t-a-t-u-2003.*

So, what made a song and music video like this so dangerous in 2002? This video intentionally showed two underage girls in skimpy private school skirts in the rain kissing. In the director's mind, he wanted soft underage porn available on every music station across the world. The two stars, both straight, planted seeds of doubt in thousands of girls across the nations. They received an outpouring of mail that this video pulled out something that was on the inside of curious young girls, including myself. Or could it be that the Enemy had strategically placed this idea into mainstream media in order to undermine the original plans of God for a family unit. In (Genesis 2:24), it says, **"This is why a man leaves his father and mother and bonds to his wife, and they become one flesh"** (CSB).

"Culturevated"

God's plan 100 percent of the time as recorded in the Bible for sex is a husband and wife—one man and one woman. That is God's best for us. In researching for this book, I came up with a term I believe to describe exactly what I experienced. I had thought it was a deadening of my senses; in fact, it is a large part of what I experienced. However, after hearing the testimony of a pastor's wife who shared that just like me she had never been attracted to women. But after watching lesbian pornography something changed on how she viewed women and sex. I can now see how lesbian thought patterns were cultivated in my mind due to the deadening of my senses. My husband is a landscaper, and cultivating the land is preparing it for a harvest. Is it not ironic that the term used for harvesting a crop where seeds are sown . . . is the same term that makes sense in my situation? My mind had been cultivated for the act of lesbianism or bisexuality as seen on T.V. I did not grow up desiring women. I had only sexually been with men, and never had given women a second look. This is where my term **"culturevated"** came from.

The first time someone even mentioned being with a woman I was 100 percent put off, disgusted, and totally told this person where to go. It was just before I met Tony. I was working at the Radisson Hotel in its restaurant. My sister, Lynn, was the manager, and I waited tables. There was also a youngish (20-something) guy who happened to be openly gay. I was all distraught over Jeff (Miles's dad) cheating on me yet again . . . I must have been crying and somehow let this guy know intimate details. FYI: Do not share intimate details with just anyone. You open the door for the Enemy to come right into your situation.

My coworker acted genuinely concerned. Without missing a beat his solution to my dilemma was to hook up with a girl. I was outraged and told him just where to go. I said, "You may like that, but I think that's disgusting, and I would NEVER be with a girl." His reply, "But it is all the same end result." So now this comment made when

I was 20 was being watered by this video I was watching when I was 24 . . . and something was starting to grow.

WISDOM ALERT
Do not share intimate details with just anyone, you open the door for the Enemy to come right into your situation.

I found myself watching this video so much that I eventually upgraded to lesbian porn. I knew it was wrong. I even hid it on my computer. But watching women seemed so much safer, softer, and more lovely. The Enemy is very crafty. If ever normal porn popped up, he would quickly remind me of the last time I was with my husband, how he forced himself on me, how helpless and hopeless I felt. I then would quickly choose the lesbian porn (as if it were safer somehow). I did not know that I was reprogramming my mind. As Christians, we are told to reprogram our mind to undo the lies the Enemy plants . . . this is found in, (Romans 12:2): **"Do not conform to the pattern of this world, but be transformed by the renewing of your mind"** (NIV). So, in Satan's true nature, distorting everything of God, he began to rewrite how my mind looked at sex. This was the cultivating of a twisted desire of God's plan for sexuality in my life. This one seemingly harmless song started an avalanche of trouble within my soul. This seed planted would bear fruit in due season . . . and even now, sixteen years later, there are still aftereffects to those choices. I must be very aware of where I stare and what I meditate on. I have looked a few times too long even in "researching" for this book, and it has triggered something inside me. I have had to quickly confess and repent. James 5:16 says, **"Therefore, confess your sins to one another and pray for one another, so that you may be healed. The urgent request of a righteous person is very powerful in its effect"** (HCSB).

One must realize that thousands of years ago when the Bible was written, there were no "mental disorders" that were named and diagnosed like schizophrenia or split personalities. Jesus called them demons and he cast them out. He "healed" people. So, when I share about voices, and thoughts, scenes played out in my mind that are clearly not from a good Father, they have to come from somewhere. They come from the **"father of lies"** (John 8:44 HCSB)—the devil. If **"Jesus Christ is the same yesterday, today, and forever"** (Hebrews 13:8 HCSB); then those whom Jesus healed then, He can and still does heal today. Matthew 17:18 says, **"Then Jesus rebuked the demon, and it came out of him, and from that moment the boy was healed"** (HCSB). Because I try to live a life pleasing to God and stay connected to the vine, *when something tries to rise up inside of me, part of my old dead sin nature,* I rely upon the Word of God to receive my healing. This, my friend, is what the purpose of this book is about. I would be lying if I told you I do not have to still **"take every thought captive"** (2 Corinthians 10:5 NRSV). Some weeks are better than others, typically depending on who I am around and what I am putting into my mind through music, movies, and media. I just want you to know healing is possible. I want to be transparent that even in working on this book, I had to step back and do an honest inventory of why I was "justifying" looking at things I had NO BUSINESS VIEWING! When you walk with God through recovery, you focus on "triggers." You are able to take ownership for your ability to avoid situations, people, even places you have no business being around.

Trigger may not be a word you are familiar with. It is defined by Merriam-Webster as: "To cause an intense and usually negative emotional reaction in (someone)." I have learned that where my mind goes (my thoughts)—my physical body will soon follow. So, I have red flags to remind me of danger ahead. Sexual perversion is just another demon, and when you are able to identify potential triggers to wrong patterns of thinking, you, dear one, are jumping on the offensive team. This makes defense 10 times easier.

In the last year and a half of my life on drugs, the older married man who had supplied my drug habit would go to jail. It became a cold new world for Nikki. I had never paid for the Meth before. I had never been ripped off, and I never had to go looking to feed my addiction on my own. By this time, I had a substantial addiction. This left me in countless sketchy situations, surrounded by dangerous people. In the end, buying pills to feed my addiction seemed the easiest.

I was laid off in 2004, and I lived on unemployment while helping my older sister who needed to have a hysterectomy. Of course, things ended badly just a few months in because I was an addict hiding behind "pot," the socially accepted drug, and drinking. So, I moved in with my mom and got a job in a telemarketing room. There, I met a confident, cocky guy (named Rick) who caught my eye. As the old saying goes: "Birds of a feather flock together." By this stage of my addiction, I could not imagine the demons I carried around with me. He too did Meth, and I let him know I was interested. He was married also, but I had already compromised on that conviction. His wife was in prison, so somehow it was even easier to justify.

Now, the first two years of my drug addiction I was sleeping only with guys. I had a few regular men I returned to, but for the most part, it was just who I could pick up that night at the club. I shared earlier how Meth is a sexual drug, so behind closed doors, I had begun to watch what I considered to be soft porn. My husband and I had watched porn during our first marriage a time or two, and I really did not think anything of it. The music video that came out in 2002 gave me a desire to watch lesbian porn that had never been there before. I did not know what had happened. A seed planted in the beginning of my separation from my husband, watered with multiple partners, grew into secretly watching lesbian and bisexual porn while up all night on Meth—a deadly combination. These habits began to birth something two years later that I never expected.

I still remember how after the first time Rick and I were intimate, my mind was flooded with thoughts of women. This was not just watching the computer screen from behind closed doors this was looking at women in the grocery store and having thoughts of real-life sexual encounters with them. Rick later told me how his wife was bi-sexual, and how they would go to bars picking up girls for threesomes. I now know he was planting seeds, grooming me for what he wanted out of our "friends with benefits" relationship. It seemed like I took on his thoughts simply because we had become intimate. This was not God's intention for relationships. His intention was for two to become one, in covenant (not just a contract that you can easily get out of). And that covenant is until death do you part. Forever, the two become one, not multiple partners, not get a new spouse when things get hard with the one you have. There is a saying, "the grass is greener on the other side." Not true. The grass is greener where you water it!

Lesbianism

Rick and I continued our "friends with benefits relationship" on and off all through 2005. By the end of that year, I became close friends with a couple in my other sister, (Noel's) apartment complex. It was mostly just a place to hang out, smoke a little pot, drink, and play cards. It was also the first place where a bisexual woman openly pursued me. Even though she was married, her husband did not care, and we must have flirted and made innuendos for a few weeks. Eventually, intoxicated, I found myself in her bed acting out the fantasies that had been playing for the past years in my mind. The next day the strangest thing happened. It seems to me I took on her thoughts just like Rick's before. I had a newfound arrogance to my walk—a spring to my step if you will. I noticed that girls noticed me. What I may have seen before as just a glance now became lustful looks. I found myself thinking all day every day about which girls I could "turn out, to seduce into lesbianism." It was like I took on a new personality that was not even mine. I remember back in high school hearing about boys who were "sluts" and how they would look for any girl to be a notch in their belt. They intentionally would seek out virgins or girls in relationships because they liked the challenge of it all. That is the best way to describe what this lifestyle of sleeping with girls was like to me. I did not just want the easy ones; I wanted the challenge. I enjoyed the hunt and the process of turning a girl out.

This identity seemed to be taking over my mind. Reflecting now, I can see the hardening of my heart (see Romans 1:24-25) was taking place, and I did not even know it. **"So God abandoned them to do whatever shameful things their hearts desired. As a result, they did vile and degrading things with each other's bodies. They traded the truth about God for a lie. So they worshiped and served the things God created instead of the Creator himself, who is worthy of eternal praise! Amen"** (NLT). I was all about the girls. And if I thought of men, it was only how I could manipulate them by letting them watch me with girls in order to get what I wanted. It seemed like everything was climaxing for the ultimate endgame. The skies opened and I could see the vision. I would have endless women because men were weak at just the option to watch. I would set up places and scenes, and the desire to get into pornography was growing inside me at a scary rate. In 2005, the most explicit pornography was only allowed to be created in Vegas, and I had a desire to get there. Again, all these sick thoughts and plans I was trying to make, made perfect sense to my skewed thinking. Many of these ideas had run together that last year before Tony got out of prison. I just know after the first time of sleeping with a woman, it was like something took over my thought process completely. Now I know I was being invaded by demons who accessed my soul through sexual contact with others who were possessed or oppressed by demons.

I was not looking for just any girl. I picked very beautiful, feminine girls. I was not full on butch (a lesbian who dresses and behaves in a more masculine manner), but I did desire to be in control—the dominant one in the relationship. Again, I traced it all back to how helpless I felt that last night with Tony. Drunken, one night watching *Catwoman*, I did shave my hair super short like Haley Berry. Sometimes, I dressed femininely, but I often found myself in more goth type clothes, very dark, almost constantly with a dog collar around my neck. It became a game. We (other friends who were on Meth, or who were into open sexual relationships) went to the clubs in packs and made jokes about who could turn who first. One small glance of interest was all I needed from a girl before it was game on. It was a very intoxicating feeling. I can see why the LGBTQ community is so pushy. Secretly, this sin is almost like bullying in form. The sex behind it is a chemically habit-forming experience. However, the chase, the turn, the spreading of the "virus," if you will, may have been more exhilarating than any of the sex.

When you are deceived, you are believing a lie. I had bought into the lie: I was a homosexual or at the very best a bisexual. Of course, my family spoke against it, but I came back with my justifications. My mom was a Christian, and she would share her faith with anyone. The very thought of her daughter being a lesbian did not go over well. I remember having this big debate with her. I argued that my attraction to women was no different than her attraction to black men. Thinking back to that day, standing in her bedroom, I remember the pain in her eyes, how she talked of the Bible, and how it was an abomination. But to me, all the lies that the world told me just made sense. If God is a God of love, then He should understand this type of relationship makes me happy. God made me, and I thought, *He does not make mistakes. He knew what I would become. How could I help my attraction to women?* With my mother I was able to debate and reason.

A little while after I came out to my mother, I decided to tell my father too. I can only imagine how devastated my father was when I was bold enough to tell him. I think a mix of the active addiction and the times I had spent defending my position caused me to be delusional. In my mind I preplanned the debate with my dad. I was sure he would argue his viewpoint. He was part of the Lutheran split when they divided over allowing homosexuals in the pulpit. My dad was vocally against gays. I still remember the look on his face when I told him I was no longer interested in men. He was dumbfounded. He would not even argue with me. The silence hurt more than any words. How could I be so disrespectful to the man who raised me? The thing about my dad that I respect more than any other person I know is how when I was growing up, he never brought women home. He might have gone to a dance. He might have stayed at a hotel, but he never paraded women around in front of me. Not one time. EVER!

As I reflect about this season, I know my heart was not completely hardened. I knew somehow that what I was doing was not right, because I continued to hide it from my children. I imagine the life my father lived and displayed for me served as a constant reminder that I could do better. However, when shame and guilt found their way in, I quickly silenced their voices, any voices of reason, with drugs, sex, and alcohol.

Over the next six months, I had multiple lovers—both men and women. I found myself going to the gay bar downtown for hook ups, and to Club 222 which was a swinger's club open only one Saturday a month. Because of my desire to still do Meth, I had now found a few more Meth cooks who had me running all over town, to Kentucky, and even to Illinois to buy pills. I have always had a business mind. I have been blessed with the ability to make connections, conduct sales, and have vision. Drugs, sex, swingers clubs, travel, buying pills to cook Meth, making, and distributing Meth, getting girls high, more sex, let me say… all of this was an EVIL combination, and a lot of bad seeds were being sown in my heart.

I had vision. At the end of February 2006 when I got my tax return, I had put together a business plan with a few different friends and guys who cooked dope. I planned to buy into a home business called passion parties, which sells adult toys, etc. Since there were hundreds of swingers clubs across the country, I planned to travel with one or two friends, hit up the clubs to sell my toys and participate in whatever ungodly things may have been going on. I would buy pills the whole way there and the whole way back. I received my toys by the end of March, and for whatever reason I went only to the club in Evansville. For the life of me, I do not know what stopped me from hitting the highway other than Tony's prayers from inside the prison. Tony told me multiple times every week the Holy Spirit woke him up to pray for me, and that he would have strong unctions all throughout the day to pray for me. In the dead of night, he would just start praying in tongues knowing **"sin was crouching at [my] door"** (Genesis 4:7 NLT).

I recall one night leaving the gay bar that was about four blocks from the downtown police station. There were four of us girls who were out for a good time. With a few drinks in me (surely enough to be charged with a DUI), I hopped in the driver's seat and began to pull off, only to have flashing lights pull me over. As the cop began walking up to the car, we all started to panic. We had a tremendous number of drugs and paraphernalia on us. I would blow dirty on a breathalyzer. As the officer took my license back to his car, the panic rose. Before we had a chance to do anything stupid, the officer and his partner went to the backs of their car and popped the trunk. I had never seen anything like this. They pulled out huge guns and came quickly to my car. I was confused and scared out of my wits. The officer threw my license into my lap and said: "It must be your lucky day. We just got another call. GO HOME!" And he ran back to his squad car and peeled out. Just dumbfounded, all of us girls started acting foolishly, like we had just gotten ourselves out of that pickle. Where would we go to get high again? That whole experience was like a buzz kill!

Can you see the delusion? God's grace and mercy stopped me from being arrested dozens of times, and who knows the countless situations I was protected from while Tony was up in the middle of the night praying over me.

Another night, after being up for a few days, I started to hallucinate. I decided to go on the hunt for more drugs instead of just going to sleep. That is the thing about my years of drug use when I thought I was a functioning addict. Because of my job in corporate America, I never stayed up more than three days. I had to sleep at least one time in the middle of the week; or when I talked, my words would not make sense. But the last year and a half of my drug use, there were no rules. I did not have a safe, secure drug hookup, and I was sketchy about what I was willing to do to alter my mind. One night I showed up to the house where the party was supposed to be. I found out they just needed me and my car to drive them to the pickup. Unfortunately, this was not just a pickup. It was a breaking and entering to steal from a dope man who was passed out asleep. I just wanted to cry, to run, to hide. I have never been so scared and worried in my life. I crossed my arms while walking through the house making sure not to touch anything. I probably was praying the whole time, but I cannot remember. I just remember going home, and how I was never willing to go to that house around that group of people again. They scared me.

I recall one time when the money was gone, and I could not even afford a bottle of gin to alter my state of mind. I was fresh out of pot, and with no dope to be found anywhere. I suddenly had a great idea: We (Rick and I) had been putting embalming fluid on our marijuana to make it more potent. I thought if I broke apart a cigarette, and sprayed the nicotine, it would give me a buzz. However, it made me puke. I did not have the patience to wait for the fluid to dry, and I almost lit my face on fire. It burned my throat so badly going down that I puked immediately. I knew that was not how I would be getting a buzz that day. This certainly illustrates how dead I was on the inside. I was willing to consume something used for dead bodies and put it into my dead, cold, shell of a body. I wanted anything just to try to alter my state of mind.

It is bizarre the ideas we come up with in our

lunacy; but when looking back I see where I was nothing more than a pawn in Satan's game. In those last few months before Tony's release from prison, I believed I was this enlightened woman who everyone wished they could be, or be with. Pride... I was so full of pride. The sexual dysfunction of my life and my openness in having multiple ongoing relationships made a few people think "they would be the one to tame the untamable." However, I was so broken from my divorce and being cheated on, I swore off commitment, monogamy, and anything that resembled a God-ordained relationship.

The Big Love T.V. series came out in March of 2006. By now I had multiple girlfriends and a man friend or two I would visit on occasion. I was a full-blown entrepreneur (openly selling adult toys and gathering pills so my friends could make Meth). I was getting more involved than ever before in the dope game. The T.V. show brought out a side of my flesh I am ashamed to reveal now. I thought I was the female version of Hugh Heffner. I wanted multiple wives. I thought about moving to Salt Lake City, Utah, but at that time, homosexual marriages were not recognized, thank the good Lord. I would watch the show and literally desire to have a life with multiple wives.

Side note: Just because it is legal, does not make it moral or right.

But, let's face it, girls are dramatic! I can even remember one girlfriend who left her ponytail holders in my car for a different girlfriend to find.

Remember my hair was short so they would obviously not be mine! I laughed about it then, how one girl thought she could make the other one break up with me. Oh, but I was honest with them all. I had had my heart broken, and from now on, I was in it for me!

My sister lived in this building, and I liked the floor plan layout. It gave me visions of grandeur. It had separate apartments (just two to a floor), four stories high. I could envision that I would eventually make so much money on the dope game, selling toys, and traveling to swingers clubs that I could buy a building and house all my different women. I would house my girlfriends who liked to drink on the first floor, the ones into coke or ecstasy on the second, on the third floor would be where I would keep my stoner girls, and on the fourth floor, well that would be where the Meth girls would go. When you cook Meth, it is normally the smell of smoking it off that gets you caught by the police. But if I owned the building, I could go to the top floor to smoke off a jar when I needed more dope. Well, there you have it, folks, a genius plan until you think about how all drugs are illegal, and I am not sure how I thought I was above the law. I could laugh or cry writing this. I was so deceived, and when you are deceived, there is a part of you that believes every single lie.

I had been looking into the porn industry. I knew at that time (in 2005–2006) you could only film explicit porn in Las Vegas and someplace in Florida. Since polygamy was illegal in all states except Utah where you could be married and still have live-in spouses, my sick twisted mind had plans to move to the southwest corner of Utah to be close enough to Las Vegas to "commute for work." I really believed that I was "a force to be reckoned with."

Looking back, I see how pivotal those few months were in my life. During February, March, and April, Satan was slinging seeds of darkness left and right. I had no idea of the power of my words, and how I was watering those dark seeds. In fact, when I would go to the swingers club in Evansville to hook up, I would also talk up my plans. Everyone saw the vision and could not wait for me to get things started so they could join me. We joked about going to hell in a bus and who we could take with us. One friend that I met at my job at OneStar (I used to call her the evil lesbian because she was an "open swinger") would be at this club many Saturday nights. It all seemed so evil how we so openly paraded around our sin, but now ten years later, I look at how different things are. This friend who worked at corporate America with me, who became a partner in crime, has since remarried and accepted Jesus as her Lord and Savior. She is now one of my go-to Christian friends, and we look back in amazement at what grace has saved us from!

Recently, I was singing a song at church, and there is a line that says, "when I was your foe, still your love fought for me." ("Reckless Love" by Cory Asbury.) I just wept, thinking about this moment in time where I mocked God, where I openly joked about hell like it was a goal to go there. We all have gifts that have been given to us by God. It is just sad for me to see how many people I led astray. Psalm 51:13 states: **"Then I will teach the rebellious Your ways, and sinners will return to You"** (CSB). The old Nikki who was created to be a leader was being used by the Enemy to lead people to hell. This is one of the reasons I am so passionate in my call to share the love of God. I never felt worthy because of the Enemy's lies, and I know others are trapped in their bondage to sin as well. It does not have to be sex. It can be drugs, or gambling, or anger, or condemnation. Satan has tons of labels he tries to make us wear. And, I plan to do my part to destroy those labels for as many people as I can. Revelation 12:11 says, **"They conquered him by the blood of the Lamb and by the word of their testimonies"** (HCSB).

While Tony was in prison, he said that over and over God had him read the Book of Hosea in the Bible. Hosea is a love story of a prophet and the woman God chose for him—a prostitute. God uses their marriage to represent how even when Christian people turn their backs on God, like this wife did to her husband, God is faithful. Hosea fights for his wife after countless infidelities. Tony thought God was having him study this book of the Bible because he had cheated on me during our first marriage. He would soon show up at my doorstep and find out why God really had him reading that book.

Tony was released April 17, 2006, to a Salvation Army in Kankakee, Illinois. I had been telling Steven, our five-year-old, that his daddy would be coming home after Miles' birthday (on the 25). But honestly, I had no intention or desire to go looking for him.

TURNING POINT

On Friday, April 28, I got up just like any other day. I was not really sure what the day would have in store for me, but I do remember I had no drugs. Looking back, I wonder if that was the motivation behind my "girls eat girls better" shirt, to possibly seek out the dope man and offer up maybe a show with my latest live-in girlfriend. So, when I got up, I put on this shirt that up until that day I had worn only at the club. I had never worn it during the day. It was a gift from a girlfriend that, really, I wore for the response it got me more than anything. Knowing what I know about spiritual warfare now, I see how I was a puppet that morning putting that shirt on to be a discouragement to Tony. I had no idea that he was on his way to get me.

That Friday afternoon about 1:00 p.m. there was a knock at the door. As I opened the door and looked up to his face to meet his eyes, he was reading my shirt. His face had such confusion and pain at that moment. I felt compassion, and I wonder if Satan was reading the look of guilt or remorse on my face, because I was instantly bombarded with like 50 thoughts.

You better shut that door.

He is here to judge you.

You know he is a Christian now. Did you see his face? You disgust him! You disgust everyone!

If you let him in, his holier than thou attitude

is sure to make you feel like crap, and you do not even have drugs to make you feel better.

He had his chance; he blew it.

Remember how he left you high and dry.

Empty promises, that is what he has to offer you . . . empty promises.

I understand now why the Enemy did not want me to let him in. Satan studies us. Satan knew how serious Tony was. He had watched him in prison. He honestly had tried to tempt him by sending the girl he went to prison with to greet him with sex and drugs, but Tony was not having it. Tony had the restoration of our marriage on his heart and mind, and he was not going to settle for anything else. God had given him a promise, and he had held onto that promise the whole time he was in prison.

He asked if he could come in. I had three and a half years of anger, resentment, bitterness, hurt, and loneliness all built up. I felt Satan welling up inside me to tell him just what I thought. HOWEVER, by the time I had a string of hate-filled words ready to come out, there was Steven. He had heard his daddy's voice. Steven begged me to let him come in, and I just could not tell him no. I offered Tony five minutes, sure that the conversation would escalate as he was most definitely going to stand in judgment of what I had become—a lesbian. No way this Bible-quoting man would stand by while a lesbian raised his son. I had watched him fight for his other kids at just the mention of marijuana in their presence. Surely, he was not going to stand by while I slept around and was so evidently strung out on Meth. Would he find out? Did he already know I was on the needle? The thought flashed through my mind . . . Did I show track marks? It had been a week or so since I had last shot up, but after a blown vein, the evidence was there for all to see. Either way, this conversation had to happen, so I invited him into the kitchen. We sat at the table to talk.

Steven was in rare form, or maybe he was just a kid who desperately missed his daddy. I was in a different form, an evil form. I remember having no drugs, little money, and just being disgusted. Pretty sure because of Tony's new "Jesus Freak" attitude, and my lesbian shirt, I was about to hear all about God, and I was super annoyed that Steven would not leave us alone. He was jumping up and down, all over Tony. I could tell the "serious" conversation we needed to have could not start till Steven left the room, so I yelled out about four or five sentences full of venom, full of hatred, full of death to my baby boy, telling him to leave the room and shut up. There had to have been curse words every other word. I remember the look on Steven's face. Tears began to well up in his little eyes. No way am I proud, but I know Tony's heart broke even more at that moment. It is not that I was so great when we first met; but I was kind and pure, and very innocent. People would say I was very naïve and gullible, always seeing the good in people. Never would I have cursed at another person, let alone my child. I am sure God allowed Tony to feel those words like knives as a reminder that I was exactly where he had left me when he went to prison, addicted to the darkness and death.

Tony held up a finger, and asked Steven to come sit on his lap. He began rubbing his little back, petting his hair as he ran his fingers through it. He told him what a beautiful, smart, happy, good, obedient little boy he was. He told him that he really wanted to hear what he had to say, but right now, Daddy and Mommy needed to talk so he needed to be obedient and go into the other room. He told Steven that as soon as we were done, Daddy would come listen to everything he had to say. He must have told him that we loved him ten times. That stood out to me, because the selfish Tony I remembered from before would have just said, "Daddy loves you." But he kept saying, "Mommy and Daddy love you." It was like he was helping to soothe the pain I had just caused, and I did not understand why. The Tony I knew, the one Satan was sure to remind me all about, would have attacked me for such horrible parenting. But not this man. This man who sat in front of me was different.

After Steven ran off into the other room, he told me calmly how it was our job as parents to call the good out of our children, to speak life over them. I was in awe. Who was this? He then explained that the world would do a good enough job of beating our children up, and that we had to use words to build them up, calling out those good qualities we wanted to see in them. I felt like I was in the twilight zone. The love, the peace, and joy were all visible. I could see a change in Tony by the way that he spoke to me and to Steven. He had a calmness about him when my whole world was nothing but chaos. His actions, his words, and his demeanor all drew me in and made me want what he had. I knew this was real. This was not like before, when he offered me empty promises. This change could be seen and experienced. He continued to apologize for the way my life was. He was taking complete ownership of the way things were. In my mind, I blamed him a little, sure; but it was not all his fault. I had made a string of horrible choices while he was locked up. Sure, I was addicted to altering my state of mind. But why? I knew the life I was living was wrong. So instead of doing the hard work to change things, I had become accustomed to getting high to quiet the voices calling me to do better.

His words were like butter on a hot roll, and they just melted my heart. Every sentence drew me in. I wanted the calmness that he displayed. Romans 2:4 tells us, **"It's the kindness and goodness of God that leads man to repentance"** (author's paraphrase). The goodness I could see, the acts of kindness I felt in Tony's presence was the presence of God wooing me, drawing me in, causing me to want to repent, to flee from my wicked ways to have what Tony had. I had always been able to draw people into my chaos, and here was Tony, here was Jesus, and the Holy Spirit was wooing me into their peace.

There are moments in life when you know what just happened changed you forever. God changed me forever through the love and patience of my husband. That day, that moment, Tony became everything I have ever wanted or needed. He was Jesus in the flesh to me. During our first marriage, Tony was amazing, hardworking, had custody of his kids, and was a loving father and excellent lover. I really did not know anything was missing. Then of course after our separation, divorce, infidelity, drug addiction, and then his prison time, I had every chance to hear what God was doing. But I was unwilling to listen. That day, when he showed up at the house, I knew that day I wanted what he had. It was like a scene from the movie *Fireproof* when the main character says she has seen the change and she wants it too. I knew Tony was different. It was not just jailhouse religion. God had changed him. Do not get me wrong . . . no person can be your Savior. Only Jesus can save us. But people can represent Christ in such a beautiful way that it affects us eternally. That is my hope with our testimony. That you will know that Jesus used my husband's arrest to save him, and then came after me through the love of my husband and saved me too. In the words of Joseph, **"What the enemy meant for harm; God turned it for good"** (see Genesis 50:20).

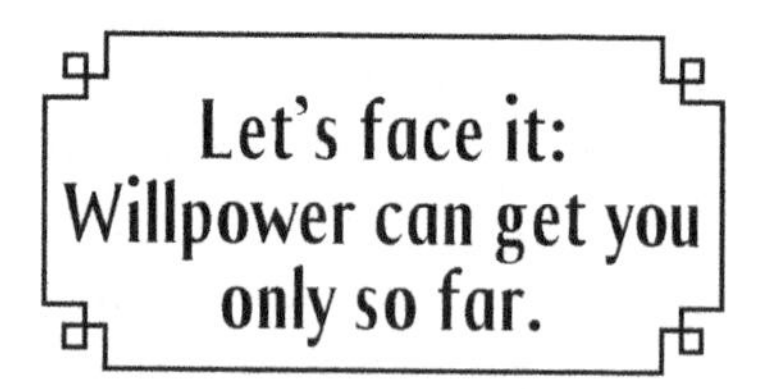

The love of a fellow Christian and seeing tangible acts of kindness was what drew me in and enabled me to walk away from a lifestyle of sex and drugs. Things didn't change immediately, and I relapsed three times after adamantly committing to be clean. I did not get addicted overnight, and I would not be changed overnight either. It would be a long road. But the decision to walk away was easy, seeing the peace and confidence that Tony had in this God with whom he was now in relationship.

I talk openly during my mentorships about what those three relapses looked like. The Bible clearly tells us what happens and why. Luke 11:25-26 and Matthew 12:44-45 both share this example: **"When you clean your house of an evil spirit, it comes out and goes into the dry arid places searching for rest. When it finds none, it comes back and finds your house clean, swept, and put in order BUT EMPTY. Then it goes and gets seven other spirits more wicked than itself and moves right in. The end condition is worse than before"** (author's paraphrase). So that is what happened to me. Every time I was with Tony, meeting the Christian people God was placing in our lives in Kankakee, I desperately wanted what he had. He tried to warn me. He explained Satan would not be happy with my choice to get clean and live right. Each time I would leave his side, I would start out strong. But that four-hour drive home is a long stretch of highway to be alone with your thoughts, especially when you know nothing about taking them captive. The phone would ring; there was a party going on; and I just needed to get there. No money was needed, and there were plenty of drugs and women to choose from. Each of those three times I made the decision to change my life for Christ, within hours I denied that choice and dove right back into my sin. I wanted out, but Satan did not want to let me go.

My story may seem like too much information. But just hold on, the key to the Scripture just quoted is to fill your house. We must put the good in. Learn a different way to cope and handle stressful situations. We must say no when even the smallest temptation comes knocking at our door. There are plenty of nuggets of truth and wisdom in the pages ahead for you to use to fight these temptations. I had to learn these truths over the past 14 years. I have placed them together for you to devour in a single evening! I love what my pastor told me: "We are the culmination of many people speaking into our lives." That is what this book represents: the truths I have been taught about my walk with God, sex, my thoughts, my marriage, effective parenting, discipleship, and the dangers that live on the other side of our computers.

In my early days as a Christian, weeks after Tony showing up in my life again, Tony began explaining how I needed to renew my mind. The book, *Battlefield of the Mind* by Joyce Meyer,[3] was one of the first books I read. Learning that Satan had been studying me, was scared of me, wanting to destroy me from the beginning, and how he had manipulated my mind was life-changing. Most

---

[3] Joyce Meyer, *Battlefield of the Mind Bible: Renew Your Mind Through the Power of God's Word* (New York: FaithWords, 2017). "With notes, commentary, and previously unpublished insights by Joyce Meyer, this Bible is packed with features specifically designed for helping you deal with thousands of thoughts you have every day and focuses your mind to think the way God thinks." —Jacket Flap.

of these teachings of Joyce Meyer talked to me a lot about division. Again, in (John 10:10), we are told, **"The thief comes to steal, kill, and destroy"** (NIV). Do you understand how he does that?—DIVISION. **"A house divided . . . cannot stand"** (Mark 3:25 NASB).

This is what is happening in our world, in our homes, and sadly in our churches. Early on in my walk with Christ, I asked Him, and I continue to ask Him to give me a heart that breaks for what breaks His. "**Break my heart for what breaks yours"** (see Matthew 5:4). For years I have been very selective about opening up about those three and a half years when my husband and I were divorced, how badly I was strung out on Meth, the lengths a girl goes to for drugs, and the sexual wickedness that grows darker and darker. Many times, I thanked God that the dealers I met in other people's homes never came to mine. I saw how they looked at the young girls of my good friends. You sweep it under the rug and say no way, they would never want a child, or she would never offer her child. But have you read the newspapers? This is happening, and no one is willing to talk about it.

Chapter 4

Let Me Reintroduce Myself: The New Nikki

I never thought I would be in full-time ministry like I am today. Some fourteen years ago, this "church thing" was simply something I looked at as a possible way out of the chaos in which I was living. I was miserable. In the depths of addiction, I think everyone gets to a place where the shameful thoughts are so loud you continually try to silence them with drugs. We call it numbing the pain in Celebrate Recovery. To see Tony so filled with life, and joy . . . but most of all peace, I had to try his way.

Basically, I could not imagine my life becoming any worse with Jesus. There is a saying out there, "Give Jesus a try. If it doesn't work out, Satan will always take you back." I think I was at that place where I had to try something . . . anything. That Nikki—the Nikki of May 2006, was headed for destruction. And unfortunately, she was taking as many people with her as she could.

Today, as I begin putting pen to paper on probably one of the scariest most controversial topics, I ask myself, *"Why me"?*

God reminds me, "**Those who have been forgiven much, love much.**" The HCSB translation of Luke 7:47 reads: "**Therefore I tell you, her many sins have been forgiven; that's why she loved much. But the one who is forgiven little, loves little.**" When I think back to the life I was living and the passion and effort I put into that lifestyle, how could I not be sold out for Jesus? What right do I have to keep to myself the miracles God has performed in my life? If I was willing to invite people on my path to destruction, then should I not be even more willing to show them the right way—the way of everlasting life? How can I enjoy life here on this earth? After learning the depths of Jesus's love for me, even though my sin was horrible, He still died for me. I cannot just stand by and keep watching children being indoctrinated into this sex-crazed culture. I cannot sit silently as I have brothers and sisters in Christ struggling with the same sex attraction and the judgment and condemnation that prevents them from the freedom Jesus died for them to have. I can no longer be ashamed or fearful about sharing the whole truth of my past and how Jesus forgave it all. I enjoy a beautiful, thriving, healthy, monogamous marriage—fourteen years and counting! I have thought about these things—over and over and over. It is time for the lies to be exposed! So, I have begun to explain the sins that once entangled me. I never want to glorify my sin; I simply want to help others avoid the temptations that are destroying so many of our families. Simply put, because I have been forgiven of so much, my heart can no longer sit by and watch how the Enemy has so many Christians cowering around the topics of sexual sin, homosexuality, and the church.

Currently (2020), my husband, Tony, and I are the directors of a Celebrate Recovery in Madisonville, KY. Over the past 14 years, we have followed the call of God on our lives from St. Anne, IL, to New Orleans, LA, and now in Madisonville, KY.

In the beginning (2006), my part of this new Christian life consisted of submitting to my husband, raising our children, and being an involved mom. Basically, I began by just sitting in a pew on Sundays and Wednesdays and trying to be a good person. My husband was audaciously on fire for God. He spoke with us daily about the power of our words, the fruit of the Spirit, and what you put in will come out. Not a day went by that he did not quote Scripture and have an explanation of why we needed to change something or improve in some way. From the beginning, we diligently guarded our home by being very careful about what people, games, music, and TV we allowed in. The transition was fairly easy for the boys, John, then 10, Miles 9, and Steven, 5 years old. St. Anne was a small town. We became active in a local Methodist Church, and God quickly began to open doors to provide for all our needs. With Tony's leadership, the transition from a worldly (negative) mindset to a positive Christ-honoring one came naturally. As Tony quoted Scripture at every good thing that happened, even what seemed to be the smallest occurrence, he was able to remind us daily of the attitude of our hearts. I lived off his faith those first few years. He has been my biggest support in my walk with the Lord. We have managed to keep an attitude of gratitude over the past 14 years that leaves some people annoyed at our joyful hearts. Do not get me wrong. We have endured our share of trials. However, if God is real and His promises are true, then why would I allow anything to steal my joy?

This "confession," if you will, is something I struggled with even sharing, but here goes. A hard truth for believers and nonbelievers both is **"the thorn in your side."** Over the years in Celebrate Recovery, I have encountered people who have gone to the altar; and the taste for drinking, or drugs, or sex has just been taken from them. They no longer struggle, or they do not admit that they struggle. I did not want to admit that I still struggle. And as I was going through this journey in the early walk of my sobriety and marriage, I let no one know the thoughts that plagued my head. In 2 Corinthians 12:7-9, Paul tells us:

> **Especially because of the extraordinary revelations. Therefore, so that I would not exalt myself, a thorn in the flesh was given to me, a messenger of Satan to torment me so I would not exalt myself. Concerning this, I pleaded with the Lord three times to take it away from me. But He said to me, "My grace is sufficient for you, for power is perfected in weakness"** (HCSB).

This today has a very different meaning than it did while I was going through it.

What was I going through . . . well, because of my intimacy with those women, I found myself fantasizing about them while making love to my husband. While my husband would be intentional about pleasing me, my mind would race with past experiences and pornographic scenes I had watched with past girlfriends.

Because I was ashamed and did not want to hurt my husband, the Enemy used this to cause a wedge in my marriage. I locked up, did not want to be intimate. Part of who God created Tony to be as a man is someone who enjoys sexual interaction very frequently. I did not always rise to my role as his wife to provide for his needs in this area. I am so sad to say that until the past five or six years, I did not see my job as his wife as the only person who can minister to my husband in this way; so of course, the Enemy tried to shut down our sex life.

My mind bothered me. It betrayed me. I loved my husband. But going back to that whole idea that when you go to the altar and get saved, they say ... go and sin no more. I did not know what that looked like. And honestly, with a sexual history like mine, I would have never felt comfortable going to anyone about it in the church. The difference between 2006 in the church and 2020 . . . is that pastors are coming out and speaking against porn. They are sharing that it is our job as believers "**to take every thought captive and bring it into the obedience of God's Word**" (see 2 Corinthians 10:5). Why then, when my husband would want to make love, was it such a fight? Because my mind was a garbage dump. Even though I was putting only good in (good tv, good movies, good music) . . . as long as Satan could get me to replay those memories every time my husband and I made love . . . or at least once a week, that fire of destructive and confusing desires kept burning on the inside of me.

In 2008, when we were making a normal trip to Evansville (a four-hour drive from Kankakee), I started having all these thoughts about drug use seemingly out of the blue. I had been clean for two years and had not even really thought about drugs. In my mind, I did battle with Satan. My thoughts were, *"I'm a Christian; I love God; I love my family, my husband, and my kids. I WILL NOT DO DRUGS."*

I only "thought" these statements, much like the sexual encounters I would replay in my mind . . . just thinking them. But a few years later, I shared this experience with a godly mentor, Ms. Dorothy. She explained why doing battle in your mind only will never work. Satan is not all-knowing like God the Father. He cannot hear our thoughts. He can only see the look on our face or our reaction when he hands us a thought. So, even though I was thinking *"I will not do drugs,"* because who says out loud in the middle of a car ride, "I will not do drugs"? What would my kids have thought? I had no idea how serious the spiritual warfare was. Ms. Dorothy explained this is how we take captive these thoughts—by bringing them into the obedience of God's Word. **We MUST quote scripture out loud over the situation!** Hebrews 4:12 tells us: **"For the word of God is living and effective and sharper than any double-edged sword, penetrating as far as the separation of soul and spirit, joints and**

marrow. It is able to judge the ideas and thoughts of the heart." I think maybe a year later we were listening to an audio tape and the book talked about how Satan watches your every move, and he sees your reaction to an attractive guy if you look twice. This, coupled with the *Fireproof* movie, and being intentional about keeping my marriage strong is when I started calling out my husband's name during love making. I remember in a teaching by Joyce Meyer, she said something like, "Think a thought, now count to ten, and keep thinking the same thought."[1] You cannot. You can focus only on the thing you are speaking. She often talks about how to change "stinkin thinkin." If I intentionally focus on my husband, on pleasing him, on saying his name, and being present . . . Satan sees my marriage is united. The thoughts must go, and my encounter with my husband is more meaningful than ever.

I have applied this same logic when Anthony and I are in a disagreement, and I hear Satan inside my head trying to get me to stage an argument or to say something disrespectful. I often just say, "I love you, Tony," first-off to defuse the situation. As the wife, I set the tone of our home. I can help keep it calm or fall for the Enemy's lies and join in the argument. I defuse the situation with a loud verbal affirmation of my love. The second reason for this is to show Satan I will not say the negative things he

---

[1] Joyce Meyer Ministries, *Enjoying Everyday Life* (Fenton, MO: Joyce Meyer Ministries, 2004).

wants me to verbalize. I imagine when I say loving words that I'm giving Satan a black eye. No, Satan, I will not give the negativity or disunity a foothold in my marriage.

When I am experiencing an intense amount of spiritual warfare around my marriage, I cling to this. I see it as kind of a secret place for me and God. Only God really knows my thought life. So, when I am in a real battle with my husband, and I am really struggling with submission to his authority, sometimes I look up to heaven and THINK: *God you know how hard this is, but I love You and I want to please YOU, so I am going to walk away from this fight. I am not going to push for my own way, because I love You; and you tell me to love and submit to my husband. God help me please, Amen.*

It is like my own silent prayer to God because Satan cannot hear my thoughts. I do not want to fight in my marriage. I want to please God. This is how I ask for help, and I will not say something I will regret. Now remember . . . I did not know any of this my first four or five years of remarriage because I was just sitting on a pew not putting any effort into growing my relationship with Christ. I am still a work in progress, but I want you to learn from my mistakes. So much of my growth has been my willingness to seek out knowledge from otherwise leaders, pastors, other Christians, and likeminded people. I commend you for taking the time to read this story of redemption!

In the beginning of our remarriage, I could recall hundreds of stories of how God showed up and out; but my work cleaning for several local doctors was one of the largest blessings for our family on many levels. The way God opened the door was quite amazing. When Tony paroled out of prison in 2006 to the Salvation Army in Kankakee Il, a man by the name of Gary would come pick up day laborers to cut down trees. Tony initially lived in the homeless shelter without us for the first month as he prepared a home for us. Tony had tree-climbing and cutting experience and he has always had a great work ethic. Gary hired Tony after his first day on the job and gave him a $2 raise, which increased his pay to $12 per hour. When the boys finished their year of school, I moved up to join Tony. ***Side Note: I have been completely free from Methamphetamine since Memorial Day, May 29, 2006.*** Tony got Gary to give me a chance as well. I was paid $10 an hour, and this allowed me to be with Tony all the time, especially as I was coming off the drugs. Gary allowed the boys to come haul off limbs and Tony paid them a few dollars each day as they helped. At one of the job sites, I needed to use the restroom. Of course, the boys all just peed in the bed of the dump truck. I was not up for that, so I knocked on the door of the homeowner. She graciously let me come in, and after I used the bathroom, she commented on how hard a worker I was, and asked if I ever cleaned homes? I answered, "Why yes" . . . thinking to myself how I cleaned my own home. This began my work cleaning houses. I was able to make up my own hours, bring Steven (our youngest) when school was out, listen to Christian worship music through a headset, and contribute to our finances. Looking back at the million-dollar homes I cleaned, only God could open a door for a 30-day clean Meth addict to have full access to these homes. In addition, I was entrusted with keys to their penthouse condos in Chicago to go clean as well. I am still amazed.

Starting Our Own Business

After nine months of working for Gary, Tony and I made plans to start a lawn care service. We would use our tax return from that year to buy the equipment. Tony had a route already established with all the homes I cleaned. Unfortunately, in 2007, our tax return was taken by the IRS for a mistake from 2001 (during our first marriage before Jesus) that we were unaware of due to Tony's incarceration. I, of course, was devastated; however, my husband amazes me with his faith. He suggested we approach one of the families I cleaned for and ask them to lend us the money to buy the mower we needed then to allow us to work it off. Without hesitation, they wrote us a $2,500 check. I remember Tony saying it was because "**God holds the hearts of kings and queens in His hand, and He turns them whichever way He wants**" (see Proverbs 21:1). Tony also explained not only to me, but also to our boys what a good God we serve and how many Christians "**have not because they ask not**" (James 4:2 KJV). Countless times, I have witnessed God come through on behalf of our family.

In 2009, when both older boys were in middle school, we started attending a larger church. It had a growing and active youth group, giving the boys new friends whose parents had similar views as we had, and giving them opportunities to do new things. We became involved in their Junior High Youth group and continued growing in Christ as a family. We had already decided against public high school after a seminar we attended at church. It explained the limited amount of time we have to make a lasting impact on our children for Christ. Homeschool seemed to be the option, until God opened the door for John to attend a local Christian school.

Throughout the years, God has placed many Christian influences in our lives. One of my most wonderful mentors from the beginning of my walk with Christ was a lady I cleaned for, Ms. Dorothy (I mentioned her earlier). We attended the same church, so she quickly got to know all the boys. She inspired me with her insight and poured love and blessings into my family. John spent time picking berries with her, and she became fond of him. She recognized that he was different than most boys his age and knew he had a call from God on his life.

When Tony's older son, Reed, from a previous marriage moved in with us, he had trouble acclimating to small-town middle school life. I needed to homeschool him. Many times, I had confided in her the struggle of getting him to complete his daily assignments when it seemed like he had given up. She sent the movie *Gifted Hands* home with us. The focus of the movie is that it is never too late. We had hoped it would be an encouragement for Reed to work toward going to high school or getting his GED. However, this testimony of Dr. Ben

John and Ms. Dorothy
at Olivet for
Dr. Ben Carson's lecture.

Carson's life assisted to inspire our son John with his dream of one day becoming a doctor. In 2012, Ms. Dorothy would even accompany John to meet Dr. Ben Carson in person as he spoke at Olivet, the local Christian College in Bourbonnais.

I used Ms. Dorothy as a sounding board and for wise counsel. As John was graduating from the eighth grade, a decision needed to be made. The homeschooling curriculum I wanted was $1500 per year and Christian school tuition was $3500 per year. It was the monthly tuition that concerned us the most about sending John to the private school. It was a big commitment. Ms. Dorothy had been praying about our situation and offered to increase my hours to cover the $450 per month tuition fee. She reminded me that John had a great call on his life and that we needed to cultivate a positive, Christ-centered environment for him as long as we could.

So, fall of 2010 John started at KTA. I volunteered at the school every opportunity I had. Being around so many like-minded Christians and amazing teachers was a dream come true for all of us. Of course, by spring 2011 with Miles' eighth-grade graduation right around the corner, we had a decision to make about Miles and Steven, our soon-to-be fifth grader. After experiencing such peace, knowing that at this school our children would be prayed over, learning the Bible daily, and in smaller classes, we just knew we had to send Miles and Steven as well. We stepped out in faith and paid the enrolment fee for all three boys, having no way of knowing how we could ever afford to pay $1,350 per month in tuition.

That summer we put in many volunteer hours helping to renovate the new building the school had purchased. The school came with 10 acres of grass that needed to be cut, as well as a parking lot that would need to be plowed in the winter. We knew that the school paid $15,000 per year for lawn care and snow removal, and that was right up our alley. So, yet again, we made our need known. We bartered a deal to take over the outside landscaping in exchange for all three boys' tuition. The mower we had would easily take 8 to 10 hours to cut the grass, so we began looking to upgrade. God opened the door with a brand new Dixie chopper on payments for two years, no interest. And just so we knew it was God, so there would be no mistake about who was in control all along, our mower payments were $450 exactly. Do you see it? That is what we had been paying the whole year before for John's tuition, and now it would cover the cost of all three boys' tuition.

At this time, I was also doing home health care for a lovely lady named Mrs. Cindy. I was content with this season of my life having work and all three boys at the same school. I had even talked Tony into going to college to pursue a degree in the arts that he could use toward a clergy degree. Sometimes, you will hear Christians say, "Don't get ahead of God, you will birth an Ishmael." The idea of Tony going to college was me manipulating Tony and birthing an Ishmael. Even though I was content, I could see how Tony was restless, wanting something more. God had not told Tony to go to college. This was Nikki trying to make something happen.

I started listening to Joyce Meyers regularly. I often share her quote: "You can be pitiful, or you can be powerful, but you can't be both."[2] She would always share what a nag she was to her husband. Her conversations were always about the things Dave needed to do to get better. It is funny, because I acted holier than thou and was very judgmental about Tony and the time he spent on Facebook. I remember driving home listening to a sermon on CD and then pulling over to get on Facebook to see just how much Tony had been online versus not doing his homework. Trust me, this approach never motivated him—not once. Joyce Meyer has always been a huge spiritual mentor to me in my walk with the Lord. She is so down to earth, relatable, and easy to understand. My heart's desire is to see people enjoy life here on earth, and that is her ministry.

---

[2] Joyce Meyer, "Joyce Meyer TV program."

My faith really began to grow. I started participating in small groups, began sharing my testimony of freedom from Methamphetamine and how God restored our marriage after three and a half years of being divorced. Meanwhile, Tony was restless. I was unaware that Tony had been praying and asking God for direction. Had he missed his call? When was God going to use him? Is this all God was calling him to, a life of cutting grass? Crazy how God's timing is so perfect. That winter we had no snow all season, and money was tight. Tony received a call from an old friend of ours from Evansville (Rob). He wanted to know if we would be interested in planting a church in New Orleans. Tony was elated, and said yes, yes, yes! Rob asked him to pray about it and to talk it over with me. Tony explained to him how just days before he had been praying, and he knew this call was the answer to those prayers. Tony was so excited. He was completely willing to step out in faith and move us almost 900 miles south—so much farther away than the four and a half hour drive to family in Evansville, or seven-hour drive to visit my dad and family in MN. This would be a huge step away from all our family. It would be far from everything we knew, and everything I had become comfortable with. So, as you can guess, I was not excited, let alone willing, to move. Tony kept saying it was God's will. He had been praying, and he just knew this was what we were destined to do. I could not imagine why God would be calling us to leave our safe little Christian community. Why would we leave? We had the school, church, income, and friends. None of it made any sense to me. At the very thought of New Orleans, I felt sick. It was sin city . . . and all I could see was a place that would corrupt my boys. NO WAY!

Tony knew he would just have to wait for God to speak to me. He had no idea how Satan was sending so many negative thoughts my way. Many of my Christian friends were encouraging me to stand my ground and not to move. A few of the women I cleaned for also wanted me to stay. Our 16-year-old John had a girlfriend, school, friends, and a life plan. Relocating was not part of that plan. John became very indignant /outspoken wanting us to emancipate him and leave him behind. All of these outside influences were giving me advice and opinions on the situation I was in. I began meditating on arguments with Tony in my mind. I would preplan rebuttals on why we needed to stay in the safety of our community. When you continually think about something... **"out of the abundance of the heart, [the] mouth speaks"** (Luke 6:45 ESV), those thoughts start to come out in actual words. We have had disagreements before, but this was different. I was being manipulated by the Enemy. I was not controlling my thoughts or **"taking them captive,"** (see 2 Corinthians 10:5). We disagreed for about two

I want you to understand that just because it sounds spiritual, does not mean it is always from God.

weeks, and the climax was when I realized Tony was not budging. He had every intention of following "Rob," our friend who really was the voice of God to us at this time. I was just unwilling to admit it. I started contemplating a separation, and I even at one time asked Tony to just divorce me. I thought I would stay with the boys in Kankakee and take over cutting the grass. He could go plant his church. It sounds foolish now. What "Christian school" would barter with me when I left my husband because he went to plant a church? After that argument, I felt sick to my stomach. I knew I needed sound advice from outside our immediate circle. Our friends and family were not bad people because they wanted us to stay. We were hard workers and brought a lot of value to the table. Some of what they said really seemed to make sense. Take my church friend Ms. Dorothy for instance. Steven had made the cover of the newspaper for the grand opening of the new school grounds, the ones we got the contract to mow and plow for. Ms. Dorothy asked me if I really believed God would call me to uproot my family from a place where God had obviously blessed us, where he had opened so many doors, and even our children had found favor? These friends of ours were not at a place where they would trust God to provide new friends, new workers, new classmates, new caregivers, new groundskeepers, etc.

Needing sound advice, I reached out to a pastor's wife. I went over all my feelings and explained everything, expecting comfort and compassion. I was looking for closure, someone to approve of the plan I had come up with which I had zero peace. Have you noticed how we do that many times as Christians? We come up with a plan of our own and then want God to bless it. I wanted her to be the voice of God telling me I was in the right, to stand my ground and all would work out. That would not be her. She grabbed me by the shoulders and physically shook my body. She asked me if I was hearing the words I was saying? Well, that was an odd question. I am sure the dumbfounded look is what led to the following questions. We sat down, and she asked me, "Nikki, have you prayed and asked God what He wants? It sounds like you have just been getting people's opinions, but what about what God wants?" Then she asked me, "When was the last time I prayed for my marriage? Or for my husband?" I felt so small. I love my husband, but I had never prayed for him. He spent years praying for me, and I never thought to return the favor. She handed me a Stormie Omartian book, *Power of a Praying Wife.*[3] She told me to spend the next two weeks praying for Tony and journal what God was speaking to me. It took only four days for God to confirm I needed to support my husband and at least go and check out the new opportunity.

At the same time this was going on, I had started my second Bible study at College Church called *Sun, Stand Still* by Steven Furtick.[4] I was

---

[3] Stormie Omartian, *The Power of a Praying Wife* (Eugene, OR: Harvest House, 1997).

having conflicting feelings about New Orleans . . . and it had only been about two or three weeks since we found out it was even on the table. Basically, I was noticing that what my friends were saying sounded selfish but also logical. The same week I started praying for my husband, week two or three of my Bible study, there was a sentence in Steven Furtick's book that really struck a chord with me. He said, "We Christians can't sit in our basement eating our can of beanie weenies waiting for the world to end. We must go share the gospel. If we do not, who will?"[5]

During that time of praying for my husband, I was cleaning for Ms. Dorothy and we were listening to a testimony via cassette tape. About 99 percent of the time she would be playing a Christian book on CD that she picked up from the library or a sermon. Remember, this was 2012. There were no podcasts yet. To this day, what she taught me about "**meditating on things that are true, noble, and just, things that are pure, lovely, and of good report**" (see Philippians 4:8) . . . think on things that are pure, holy, and lovely, is something I practice every day. Just like we did everyday cleaning,

---

[4] Steven Furtick, *Sun Sand Still: What Happens When You Dare to Ask God for the Impossible* (Colorado Springs, CO: Multnomah Books, 2010). Steven Furtick challenges you to believe that the audacious faith that we see in the Bible, the faith that caused a man to pray and see the sun stand still in the sky, is the same faith we can claim for ourselves today.

—From publisher's description

I listen to audio books on my phone every day, podcasts sometimes, and worship as well through a headset. Every day, without fail, I put these good things in. This particular day with her, she had put in a cassette tape about a mistreated son to a missionary man. He had been horribly physically abused till his dad was incarcerated, who then had an encounter with Christ and became a missionary in the country with the largest population of orphans. He talked about that verse that says, "**many are called but few are chosen**" (Matthew 22:14 NRSV). He related it to how so many of us are called, God ordained, to go and share the gospel. But most act as if they are locked in a prison cell, paralyzed, unable to move. If they only knew that like in Matthew 22:14 Jesus opened the lock, the door is open, and we just need to get up and go. She shut the tape off at that moment and told me God had just revealed to her that our family had to go to New Orleans. With the state of Louisiana having the highest incarceration and recidivism rate in the world, they needed someone to come and share the good news. The Webster's dictionary defines *recidivism* as "a tendency to relapse into a previous condition or mode of behavior, especially relapse into criminal behavior."[6] We had overcome drugs and alcohol and God had restored our family. God had always provided financially for

---

[6] Webster's Dictionary. Accessed October 17, 2020. *http://www.m-w.com/dictionary*.

us, **"[establishing] the work of our hands"** (Psalm 90:17 ESV), despite Tony being a convicted felon. We were and are a success story for the Lord. God tells us in Revelation 12:11: **"They have overcome him by the blood of the Lamb, and by the word of their testimony"** (NKJV). This had to have been the most intense conversation I ever had with Ms. Dorothy. (I do not remember saying a word.) She was very serious about the call of God on my family's life. Then she handed me the tape to keep. I keep it as a reminder how God still speaks to us.

It is rather amazing how God works. Remember how I said we had no snow that winter? When Rob called my husband a few weeks before, we had only $40 in our bank account. Just a few days after my heart became aligned with my husband's, God dropped a 30-day, 70-hour a week head foreman job for a Barnes and Nobles right into Tony's lap. We ended up with more than $10,000 in less than a month. It was enough money for us to scout out the area that Easter over spring break, and then to make the move in June.

Chapter 5

A New Season: NOLA

As for that Easter trip, I laid out a fleece for God, asking for three things: finances, Christian schooling, and housing. God made sure to confirm He would cover all those bases for us the first 48 hours we were visiting New Orleans. We were offered a three-bedroom/2-bath house in the inner city rent free in exchange for handyman work. The school offered us the same barter deal, as the Kankakee school. I would work in the kitchen, and my husband would cut grass in exchange for $18,000 a year in tuition. And, my husband was given a position at Touch Global, an outreach ministry in Southern Louisiana.

We grew more as Christians, as a family unit, and as a husband and wife living there just a few years compared to the six-year season we spent in St. Anne. I realize a lot of my "lack of growth" in Kankakee was because I did not put forth the effort to feed my spirit. I set the pace, and it was that of a turtle those first six years. If **"faith comes by hearing, and hearing by the word of God"** (Romans 10:17 NKJV), I had limited what God could do in and through me. Simply put, I was lazy, just wanting to sit in the pew, not participate, not study, not engage, and not grow. I love what Lysa TerKerst says, "If the enemy can isolate us, he can influence us." [1] That is why we need our church community to grow. The Enemy had me believing the lie that since I was not feeding my mind garbage, and I was no longer drinking and doing drugs, I was ok. Of course, Satan wanted nothing more than for me to be a pew sitter and put nothing good into my mind and heart so I could grow.

Our first day in New Orleans, my husband experienced healing through the hands of our son Steven. Tony misstepped off the U-Haul, and Steven laid hands on his ankle and prayed. Tony was able to get up and walk, finish unpacking the truck, and participate in all that week's prayer walks. We arrived just before a youth convention where Francis Chan was the keynote speaker. More than 5,500 youth had invaded New Orleans to spread the gospel. Teams from churches hit the streets, and our group of "church planters" joined us to share the gospel in our "target market." Tony and I were able to witness our son Steven leading several

Watching our son share the Romans Road to salvation.

[1] Lysa TerKeurst, *It's Not Supposed to Be This Way: Finding Unexpected Strength When Disappointments Leave You Shattered* (Nashville: Nelson books, an imprint of Thomas Nelson, 2018).

people to Christ using an evangacube. As a mother, it still resonates as one of the proudest moments in my life!

God Meets Our Needs

Even though the initial month had supernatural victories, we also experienced spiritual battles our first nine months in the inner-city doing street ministry. Those trials brought us closer as a family and more able to appreciate how God provided one need at a time exactly when we needed it. Here are just a few of the highlights. Our bank accounts were seized for back child support. (It was the last $1,200 we had when we first moved to New Orleans.) We received a donation in the mail the very next day, a $500 check to the ministry church plant, and a $500 check for us personally. Our vehicles were vandalized (shattered windows four different times), yet God provided the finances to replace those windshields. We cleaned up the empty lot next to us, because it was the right thing to do. The owner hired us to clean up another lot, and then paid us double our invoice. There was one month when the lawn mower payment was due, immediately. I left for work telling Tony we would have to call my father about not being able to pay the loan. But God . . . Did you know that 61 times in the Bible there is a "But God," which denotes a moment in time where God intervened in a way that man could not have orchestrated even if he had wanted to? Like "But God" is that phrase that reminds you not just "but God," but ONLY God. That day we received a $1,000 check in the mail from a former boss. He included a letter that stated he had some extra money, and when he prayed, God told him to send it to us. It not only covered the $450 lawn mower payment but gave us extra money right before Christmas. Even as I type, these moments where God showed up and allowed me to relive them and stir up that faith of how God has always come through, I remember that just before the answer came, before we knew the bill would get paid, the temptation to question God was there. The temptation to step outside the will of God and try to make something happen was there. But this season in our lives, living in inner city New Orleans, was more about our learning to rely on God and trust Him in every way. Our first nine months could be described as the poorest financial season of our lives ever, and yet we never lacked or wanted for anything. God always provided! Putting this in the perspective from a numbers point of view, we lived on just $4,000 for more than nine months. Tony could make that amount in one job in less than one week in any other season of our lives. But God needed to strip away our ability to provide for ourselves so that we could trust Him, call upon Him, and grow in Him in ways we had never experienced before.

A Season of Growing

The climax of our stay on Derbigny Street would have been the Saturday before Super Bowl Sunday. I know I have told this story a hundred times, and even now eight years later, it is still very vivid in my memory. Just like any Saturday night we were in bed by 10 p.m. I am sure of this, because of church the next morning. This particular Super Bowl was being held in New Orleans, so there was a lot of traffic and roads were blocked off. We made sure to have all the supplies we needed and stayed home. About 2:00 a.m., we woke up to our car alarm going off. Twice in the past couple of months this had happened as people had thrown bricks through our car windshields in the middle of the night. As the alarms began to go off—one, then another—we heard tires screeching against the concrete. We ran from the back of the house to see what was going on. By the time we made it to the front porch, we could see a large SUV pulling

off with smoke and damage to the whole front end. Tony instinctively jumped in my minivan to chase them down. His initial thought was, "Run toward the danger." My initial thought: "Call the police." These hit and run drivers had crashed into all four of our vehicles, but then drove four more blocks without hitting another thing. They pulled over or broke down (who really knows), and they all jumped out to scatter. My husband said he picked what he believed to be the slowest one (who also happened to be the biggest one) and chased him back to the front of our house. The man was just too intoxicated to know that he was running back to the scene of the crime. By the time the night was over, we confirmed the car had full insurance coverage. Even though three of our four vehicles were declared "totaled," God used this situation to upgrade our minivan which literally was on its last leg.

This financial windfall, much like the phone call for the Barnes and Nobles job, happened "suddenly." Just like that we were above water again, in awe of how God provides.

Just a month later, Tony was blessed with a really good job. Then on the first of May, he was contracted for what we like to call "the sugar job." The job consisted of about 45 shipping containers filled with 950 – 1,000, 50-pound bags of sugar that we had to unload, palletize, and shrink wrap. The job initially was set to pay around $14k, but because we did it so well, with so little waste, in such an efficient amount of time (half the time they expected), the business owner blessed us with a

$3,800 bonus. Who does that? MY GOD! That is the God we serve; One who does not want to be put in a box and **"wants to do above all you could ever hope, dream, or ask for"** (see Ephesians 3:20).

New Orleans, for me, was the hardest yet most beautiful growing process for my walk with the Lord. New Orleans is where I started using the app on my phone called "Audible." I currently have more than 50 books that I have downloaded and listened to over the past five years. Remember, listening to pure, holy, and lovely things is a character trait Ms. Dorothy taught me early in my walk with the Lord. I love using this app, even with my husband and youngest son on road trips. This was a way for me to feed my spirit while on the go. I mostly have Christian books where preachers and speakers teach how to apply the Word of God to your daily life. *Redeeming Love* by Francine Rivers[2] is one of the few historical fiction books I have ever listened to. The story depicts a modern-day telling of Hosea (modern-day 1800s) that is. There is part of the story where the Lord had revealed how Angel had a false sense of security in her husband—she found her joy and her meaning to life in Hosea her husband, not God. In retrospect, I can see how during the first six years of my remarriage to Tony, I looked to him for all my needs, not to my Lord and Savior. I had placed my marriage above my relationship with Christ. It is in moments like

---

[2] Francine Rivers, Redeeming Love: A Novel (Colorado Springs, CO: Multnomah Books, 2007).

these, that the Holy Spirit has been able to reveal different truths to me. Previously, I had been lazy in my walk with God. This hard season of planting the church, uprooting my family, starting over, and ministering to the lost caused me to lean on Jesus, not just Tony. This grew my Christian life at a rapid rate. I am so thankful to have learned through those challenges, that my walk with God, is my responsibility. And that true joy is found in my relationship with Christ, not what my husband does or does not do for me.

After leaving the inner city of New Orleans, we bought a home on the West Bank in Westwego, just over the bridge from New Orleans. We experienced a calm season. This I can see was for our marriage to grow, and for me to spend time in God's Word learning for myself. Life was coasting along smoothly. We were yet again active in church. Tony was doing very well at his job, and financially we were very blessed. Our kids were all doing well. We felt like we were coasting, somewhat idly.

Chapter 6

A Deeper Call

The summer of 2014 started to stir something new in me with the legalization of same-sex marriage in five states, one of them being Indiana. This triggered something inside me. Indiana is where Tony and I lived during our first marriage, and after our divorce it was where I openly claimed the bisexual title. I had many friends still living there in a lifestyle of bondage. I knew of only a few of us who had made it out of that lifestyle. And several friends had died in the madness.

I remember one friend had reached out to me via Facebook, while we were still living in Kankakee. I would not become her friend online and even labeled her as the "Evil Lesbian," because we had lived that swingers' life-style together. I was afraid. As a new Christian, sometimes Christians warn you not to reach back into your old lifestyles trying to help people. After all, **"bad company ruins good manners"** (1 Corinthians 15:33 ESV). After about six months, we became friends again at a safe distance via the Internet. She had really changed. She was serving the Lord, digging into His Word, and remarried. As we both watched the instant hate and uproar at the legalization of gay marriage, we chatted often about how wrong it was and even how someone needed to do something. Now in New Orleans where "anything goes," I watched the persecution of other Christians who were standing on their religious convictions. Facebook seemed to be a hot spot to share news from all over the nation. Every other day it seemed there was a new law suit where a Christian was being persecuted for standing up for his/her religious convictions. For example, many florists and bakers who did not want to bake the cake for a homosexual wedding were taken to court and fined over their choice to deny service.

Modern-Day Persecution

With dozens of other examples out there, I have included three stories all from *LifeSite News*. On March 1, 2013, an elderly Christian by the name of Barronelle Stutzman refused to do a wedding because of her relationship with Jesus Christ.[1] She tried to be as open and honest as she could. She explained to the potential couple that her convictions and love for Jesus would not allow her to provide flowers for a gay wedding. It was the only wedding she declined in 37 years. In a court ruling, Stutzman was ordered to making a public apology, as well as donate $5,000 to a local LGBT youth center and make a promise to no longer refuse service to

---

[1] Ben Johnson, Website: *Life Site News* (8.13.2015). Court rules Christian baker cannot refuse to make wedding cake for gay "marriage."

customers based on their sexual orientation. I was convicted. Ms. Dorothy had pushed us to come to New Orleans to share the freedom and restoration of our marriage to this group of people. But was God in fact calling me out of my comfort zone to speak out about homosexuality?

In a later case, the court ruled against a Christian baker who refused to make a wedding cake in Denver, Colorado. The baker, Jack Phillips, changed his entire business model. Because of the ruling that would force him to go against his convictions, he chose to no longer make or sell wedding cakes.[2] This decision cost him 40 percent of his revenue. I am just confused about the signs I always saw growing up that any business had the right to refuse service to anyone. Why is that not still the case? People labeled with "hate crimes" are popping up everywhere.

The third story I want to share is from a standpoint that uncovers how the LGBTQ community looks for Christians and Christian-owned businesses to harass or sue and to make them an example. In Dearborn, Michigan, an undercover reporter went into several Muslim-run bakeries. There were a few who would bake a cake for a homosexual wedding, but most would not.[3] Yet that is never in

---

[2] Steven Crowder, Website: *Life Site News* (4.7.2015). Court rules Christian baker cannot refuse to make wedding cake for gay "marriage."

[3] Kirsten Anderson, Video, *Faith, Homosexuality, Marriage* (4.7.2015).

the media. Have you ever heard of a Muslim being sued by the LGBTQ? Are you aware that in Muslim run countries, homosexuals face death under Sharia law? Something was stirring wanting me to share the freedom that Christ had provided for me. Everywhere it seemed there where opinions popping up that once gay always gay. Because it was not a choice, they "deserved" their wedding cake and flowers. This growing desire to scream a different answer was boiling over inside me.

Yet again, Tony and I began a new Bible study. This is key to the strengthening of our marriage; we grow by learning the Word of God together. This time it was Francis and Lisa Chan, "You and Me in Light of Eternity."[4] They compared what your marriage looks like in the long run compared to the race we are called to run for God. We are continually called to go and share the good news, not merely make a living, become financially stable, then retire. This changed everything. Tony and I found ourselves being challenged into a new level of ministry. Could I speak to people about what marriage was supposed to look like, and how God can mend any broken heart, because He did it for us? Could I just leave that season of homosexuality out of my testimony?

We prayed and were given confirmation again and again. God had opened doors for us to relocate

---

[4] Francis Chan and Lisa Chan, *You and Me Forever: Marriage in Light of Eternity* (San Francisco, CA: Claire Love Publishing, 2014), 55.

with a place for us to stay in Kentucky (which was centrally located for us to travel). My cousins knew our heart to share what God had done and offered us a place to stay in their home. We will forever be grateful to how God used them to open the door to this season of ministry. We launched our 501(c) 3 nonprofit Prisoner2preacher ministry. We had friends and family offer for us to come share our testimony at different churches across the country. It seemed like just sharing about the healing power of Jesus would in fact be enough.

Celebrate Recovery Ministry

When we moved to Kentucky and started attending our cousins' church, the pastor asked to hear our story. He immediately asked us to consider starting a Celebrate Recovery Ministry. He explained that the city had tried before, and it had not lasted. After prayerful consideration, we decided this was a good ministry opportunity. We could still travel, and it would allow us to share, mentor, and disciple. Here we are three and a half years later, loving it.

Of course, there were several deciding factors for us to stay and put down roots in Madisonville. Several of our adult children lived in Evansville just 50 miles north. This would allow us to minister to them without moving back to Evansville. Steven was now in high school, and we were homeschooling him. Madisonville would be much smaller than New Orleans and Evansville, allowing us to feel safer with him riding his bike or running to the Y to play basketball. We had a large number of family members in the area. Soon we found an amazing house with some land with two garages for all my husband's stuff, and it was large enough to accommodate our massive family when they would come to visit. (When we purchased this place in 2017, we had 10 grandchildren from our nine kids.)

Launching the Celebrate Recovery Ministry has been a huge growth process for us as well. We enjoy the structure of the steps and how they are founded on God's Word. We know we are called to go and make disciples, and that is the number one goal of C.R. (Celebrate Recovery)—sponsors and accountability. We can mentor alongside people who are caught in tough situations and share the hope and love that is found in God's Word.

The Call—Up Close and Personal

You may be asking yourself, *why would anyone choose to write this kind of book?* Well, I have a great deal of firsthand knowledge and have seen multiple people freed from sexual sin—myself included. But I would like to share the moments leading up to my decision to tackle one of the most controversial topics today.

Our first year here in Kentucky, we became witnesses to a case of sexual child abuse and worked with Child Protective Services to have the child placed in a safe home. For more than four years being part of this process up close and personal has been the key in my decision to write this book.

My husband's past is very colorful with multiple arrests leading to short and long times in and out of jail. When we became involved with the case, we decided we would review the discovery in an effort to help understand what was going on with this family. "The Discovery" is a very detailed account of testimonies, list of evidence, dates, times, numbered accounts and so on. Basically, it is the list of evidence the prosecutor has to go on in order to process the accused. Both parents were behind bars with 81 different felony charges including rape, incest, and sodomy. After reading just the first five pages of the 45 pages of evidence, we had no doubt this dad had spent six months molesting his own daughter. Let me say again, there are things that once you see, hear, or read are imbedded in your memory; no matter how hard you try you cannot undo the dark seeds once they are sown. This is huge for me as I write this book. I never want to overshare (it sounds like I am glorifying my sin), or paint pictures for the Enemy to use against someone's mind. However, in order to understand how the Enemy is attacking our children's minds, some things have to be said. So, this discovery, this case, has haunted me and even initially affected my relationship with my husband. I do, one hundred percent, believe that when we repent and turn from our sin, we begin to plant new seeds, positive moments, and make new memories. Therefore, with time and the renewing of our minds, it does get better. But you have to be intentional, and I will talk more about that toward the end of this book.

Both parents had been behind bars for three months, and the daughter was in foster care. When family members asked me and my husband if we would get the mother's mementos from the home, we agreed. After all, she had baby books, pictures, and things that you cannot replace. Because we knew this family before the allegations, we wholeheartedly believed the mother was naïve and the father had groomed and manipulated her as well. It is so tragic that these things have happened, and we were just wanting to help the family as best we could.

It was February 2016, and it was a short drive to her home from where we lived. But this road trip would be harder for me than any other. I had really been struggling the past three months with replaying the details of the event over and over. Those sentences that I read became scenes that would play and replay in my mind. As we drove, with each mile marker we passed, my mind raced with worry and anxiety. I did not know what we would find. Our motivation was the grandfather to the abused little girl. He was so broken and just wanted help securing his grandchildren's memories.

Walking in was creepy for me. I was just so unsure. My husband, on the other hand, was openly unattached. He just kept reminding me we wanted prison ministry, and we had a job to do. It is funny how different men and women can be. He instantly began looking for pictures, baby books, and anything they might want to keep. I opened each tote like a dead body was going to jump out at me. It did not take long to start locating this precious family's valuable memories. We retrieved baby books and photo albums. (I will call the

12-year-old Jane Doe because of privacy.) Walking through the memories almost made it seem like all those gruesome details I read were not real. It was as if she were a normal 12-year-old girl without a care in the world. She wanted to play basketball or have friends come spend the night. We worked quickly to fill my husband's truck with the belongings. It was hard to pick and choose what would stay and what would go. We had limited time, space, storage, and room in the truck; so we had to open every tote and box to see if it would make the cut and get loaded onto the truck.

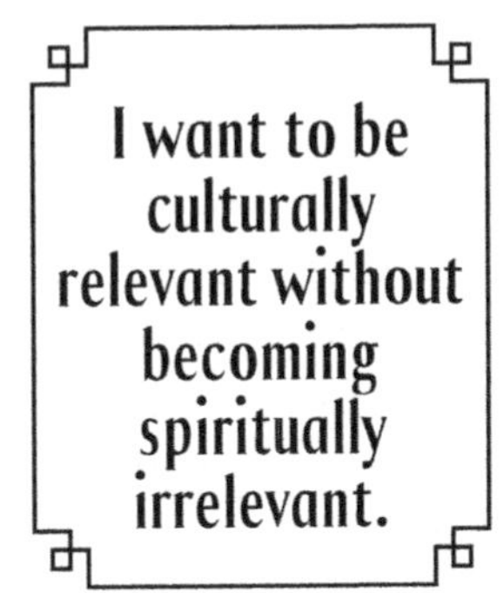

Enjoying the joy of Jane Doe's childhood memorabilia, I almost forgot why we were there. But then it happened. I came across something disturbing. Items the police had obviously overlooked. My heart sank. How could someone be so evil? How could they do those things to their own child? Almost instantly, sickness took over my body. I found myself locked in the bathroom, crying about even being in this place—the place where this little girl was violently violated. Without being able to stop, my mind went back to the discovery. And as every word, description, and phrase was replayed in my mind, I just began to bawl. I wept because I was mad and angry. Why did these things have to happen to her? And then, it was like I heard God speak audibly to me. He wanted to remind me that I was headed on a path for sexual destruction as well, and who knows where I would have ended up? God reminded me of what I was doing exactly 10 years ago. It was a painful memory, but one I had to take a long hard look at. Do you remember earlier in my story how in February 2006, just two months before Tony's release from prison, I had bought into the adult toy business? Had I not quit the drugs, remarried my first husband—a strong man of God—relocated, and gotten heavily involved in church . . . who knows where I would be? Sexual sin only gets darker, and more deviant. God was telling me had I not changed, I would have been no better. I find myself telling people every day that sin is sin, is sin, and it is all equal at the foot of the cross. However, when a child is violated something inside just screams out. Could it be that Mark 9:42 stands out? **"But whoever causes the downfall of one of these little ones who believe in Me—it would be better for him if a heavy millstone were hung around his neck and he were thrown into the sea"** (HSBC). I knew after we stumbled upon these disturbing things that light must be shed on the topic of sexual sin. But how? Why me? I love my ministry helping people overcome drug and alcohol addiction. It is safe sharing how God restored my marriage and about being a mom who prays. Indeed, I will tell anyone about that. But other sin—gross, loose-living sin—before my marriage was restored, I would rather that stay dead. Besides, I have heard how church people talk about "those" people. According to God's Word, "**I am a new creation in Christ**" (see 2 Corinthians 5:17). My sins have been nailed to the cross. But for me, it is scary sometimes to share openly, without glorifying the sin, how God has brought me out of it. Even now, as I have shared this topic, it is awkward. I must pray each time for the Holy Spirit to guard my tongue and lead my words.

Fourteen years happily remarried, faithful, and fulfilled, I want others to know this life in Christ exists. There is healing and work to do, but you can walk away from a sexually deviant lifestyle. When I heard the Holy Spirit remind me of who I once was, I knew I was not to judge but to pray for this family, even the man who was sitting behind bars. Even though I was initially very defensive about how different he was from me, and almost justifiable in my sin, God showed me otherwise. Have you ever had an "aha" moment where the light comes on and you understand what God was talking about? It was that long hard look at who I was ten years ago to the month ... it was that lifestyle I would not want to admit. I too was "out there." I was living a life of sexual promiscuity.

I have to retain a God-centered worldview at all times.

This is the motivation behind this book. It is scary for me to openly admit who I once was, and I find myself worried even now about what some people will say. But even just this morning, God reminded me through a sermon that He has a purpose for my past pains; and if I let Him remain in control, my story of redemption can help many.

When God showed me I was on a path no different than that criminal, that child molester, I had to ask myself ... *Did his parents see signs, did his parents help create this? Do we hurt our kids by allowing the LGBTQ community to bully us into silence? How should we respond when they say we are hate-filled, narrow-minded Christians who are not allowed to have an opinion about purity. Can we speak out about sexual sin without being targeted?* I want to share good and bad seeds that were planted in my mind, or were planted in front of me into the minds of my children. This will give you real life examples of what to expect. I am not the expert, and I do not claim to have all the answers, but I do know the One who does. I have sought out the Holy Spirit in writing this book that it may work alongside the Bible to help others who feel trapped, hopeless, and worthless to find the strength in Christ they need to overcome the Evil One.

Chapter 7

Seeds of Death and Seeds of Life

The purpose of my book is to equip people with tools to fight the battle that is waging against our families, especially our children. To understand this war and the Enemy's tactics is necessary to recognize how to win. The direction of our lives goes directly according to the seeds we water the most. There is an old Cherokee teaching between a grandfather and his grandson that illustrates these truths.

Two Wolves

> An old Cherokee is teaching his grandson about life. "A fight is going on inside me," he said to the boy.
>
> "It is a terrible fight, and it is between two wolves. One is evil—he is anger, envy, sorrow, regret, greed, arrogance, self-pity, guilt, resentment, inferiority, lies, false pride, superiority, and ego." He continued, "The other is good—

> he is joy, peace, love, hope, serenity, humility, kindness, benevolence, empathy, generosity, truth, compassion, and faith. The same fight is going on inside of you—and inside every other person, too."
>
> The grandson thought about it for a minute and then asked his grandfather, "Which wolf will win?"
>
> The old Cherokee simply replied, "The one you feed." [1]

The direction of our lives goes toward the seeds we water the most. I think we have underestimated our thought lives and our responsibility to control our thoughts. Our thoughts had to matter to Jesus; He said in Matthew 5:28, **"But I say to you that whoever looks at a woman to lust for her has already committed adultery with her in his heart"** (NKJV). These inner thoughts dictate the outcome of our lives. In daily conversations, I have said multiple times, "Where you stare you will steer." Lysa TerKerst writes this in her book, *It's Not Supposed to Be This Way*.[2] I've even heard different preachers say, "The voice you believe will be the future you receive."

---

[1] Billy Graham, "When the Holy Spirit Has Come," in *The Holy Spirit: Activating God's Power in Your Life* (Waco, Texas: Word Books Publisher, 1978), 33.

[2] Lysa TerKeurst, *It's Not Supposed to Be This Way* (Nashville: Thomas Nelson, 2018).

I want to challenge you. We know that **"Faith comes by hearing, and hearing by the word of God"** according to Romans 10:17 NKJV. So we grow our faith in the Word of God, but how do we grow love, compassion, and empathy? How can we supplement the **"fruit of the Spirit [which] is love, joy, peace, longsuffering, kindness, goodness, faithfulness, gentleness, and self-control?"** (Galatians 5:22-23). We do this by listening to, watching, and reading about these qualities. There are so many family-friendly shows available, entire TV stations (PureFlix) where every show has some or all of these underlining qualities. At the same time, I believe it is our job to guard our homes against the "works of the flesh." In Galatians 5:19-21, we are given a list so we can avoid the flesh and not feast on it in our living room as a family.

> **Now the works of the flesh are obvious: sexual immorality, moral impurity, promiscuity, idolatry, sorcery, hatreds, strife, jealousy outbursts of anger, selfish ambitions, dissensions, factions, envy, drunkenness, carousing, and anything similar. I tell you about these things in advance—as I told you before —that those who practice such things will not inherit the kingdom of God** (HCSB).

Those are some pretty strong words by Paul. Again, I write this book to warn and give examples of how Satan planted seeds of sexual impurity into my heart by things I watched. You may not struggle in any of these areas, and I never want to fall into legalism and a long list of do's and don'ts. I share these things because I care about the desensitizing of our youth and a vast majority of Christians who would rather entice their flesh with a NetFlix series than challenge their walk with God and dig into His Word.

I want to take some time in this chapter to give some examples from my life and parenting. I have seen the Enemy attempt to gain entry even for a moment until we discovered him, shut him out and IMMEDIATELY repented. First John 1:8-9 says, **"If we claim to be without sin, we deceive ourselves and the truth is not in us. If we confess our sins, he is faithful and just and will forgive us our sins and purify us from all unrighteousness"** (NIV). In 2016, there was a new series about to be released on Netflix! I had been waiting just like thousands of Americans for the release of this family-friendly show. I had followed the remaking of the show on Facebook and was so confident that it would be the perfect show for me to enjoy with my 16-year-old son, Steven. I would be able to tell him about the version from way back when I was a little girl, and it would become table talk for us. I think we made popcorn then sat back ready to spend the evening binge-watching together. Episodes one and two had a few racy outfits, but I quickly shrugged it off because this was supposed to be a family- friendly show. There was a super outspoken Christian on the show. Besides, the clothes they were wearing were really nothing worse than what we see in the real world. This was the first check in my spirit that I ignored. I was justifying watching things that were questionable, things I would not have sat down with my grandparents and watched. I should have turned off the television. By episode three we found them in a nightclub dressed super sexy, reenacting the scene from twenty or thirty years earlier when they were kids. Two grown, attractive women were dressed very provocatively. This version was a steamer to watch, especially different from the original dance when they were in middle school decades earlier. This new remake of the dance won them first place. As they were called to the stage to get their prize, they were described as delightful lesbians. Of course, the wording was changed. No name or exact wording could be used from the show because of copyright infringements. I was mortified. I paused for a moment; knowing what this Christian lady was going to say: "Of course we're not gay, we are just friends," to quickly cover it up, right? WRONG!

I shut the show off immediately and looked at Steven to tell him that **"we may be in this world, but we are not of this world,"** (1 John 2:15, author paraphrased). My heart ached for the millions of viewers who now have that seed planted into their hearts. Twenty-five percent of U.S. children live without their father, according to the Annie E. Casey Foundation (a philanthropic foundation, building a stronger future for deprived children).[3] Young girls and boys are being raised by a mom alone doing the best she can do. More and more, there is not a "normal" Christian home or Christian

---

[3] Annie E. Casey Foundation. https://www.aecf.org/about/.

marriage being represented. Thirty-five percent of kids are in a single-parent family home where there is minimal chance of a happy godly marriage lived out in-front of them. Biblical marriage is really a fairytale to most young adolescents. Add to that scenario arguments where mom and dad fight verbally or physically in front of these young people. Of course, they do not want that kind of relationship! When they sit down to watch what has been bragged about to be a "family-friendly show," a dark seed is planted about a homosexual relationship and how acceptable it is. This is how the desensitization of our youth happens as homosexuality is encouraged from every angle. Pause and think, or as you watch T.V. shows, commercials, even movies, homosexuality is almost always portrayed now. WHY?

When Steven was 6 or 7 years old, we were parked in the car while Tony was inside doing something. Out of the clear blue, Steven said, "Hey mom, what's a dildo?" Talk about being taken aback and shocked out of my mind. I snatched the phone out of his hand that he was playing on and immediately started asking the older children what he was playing. Now keep in mind this is a game downloaded to a phone with no Internet needed, and it is 2008 or 2009. Things are much worse now! He was playing GTA (Grand Theft Auto). Now the game is rated "M for Mature"; however, our 16-year-old had downloaded it into his phone while living in Evansville, and now he had brought it into our home. Just like that, a seed was planted. What if he had gone to the Internet to ask the question, "What's a dildo?" Parents, can you see the importance of monitoring what our children are playing, and watching, and listening to on phones, tablets, and other "screened" devices? How many devices are in your home? When your kids have headsets on, do you know what they are listening to? When is the last time you checked? I originally had an entire chapter on the billions of dollars the USA spends every year on GTA. It is a game where stealing cars, killing cops, and having sex with prostitutes are all in a normal day's play. I spent a week diving into both sides of the "justification" as to why parents of twelve and fourteen-year-olds would buy this game for their kids. Parents argue how mature their child is, and how they trust Timmy not to do the "challenge" or go into the "strip club." In case you do not know, (because I did not) when your character is injured, they get healing by having sex or getting oral sex from these prostitutes who are positioned all throughout the game. After having sex, they have the option to have more sex (which is visual as well as hearing the girl's pleasure), pay the girl, or just kill her and keep the money. So there you have it, folks. Hundreds of thousands of our youth are being introduced to pornography, violence, theft, and police hatred all through a top-selling video game.

Back in 2010, just before our move to New Orleans, we had gotten cable for the first time in five years. I remember one "Sunday Morning" lying in bed as my husband still slept and browsing through the channels. It all happened before I even realized what was going on. I recognized a star, an actress I had watched in *Dear John* and other movies I liked. I began to watch without even reading the description. Before I knew it, multiple steamy scenes began to play out before my eyes. First, the older married woman hired the young actress, I had watched in many movies before, to lure her husband in, to entrap him to see if he would cheat. First of all, this should have been a red flag for me. My husband and I have a boundary in our home. When a show, a song, or a movie shows unfaithfulness or sexual scenes, we turn it off. This is something we do to guard our hearts, and 99 percent of the time, we are very faithful to this rule. But this morning, this Sunday morning before church, I let the show stay on. I watched the entrapment, and I continued as I could tell a desire was playing out between these two women. I was all up in my flesh, excited to see what would happen next. The outside world was gone and I was zoned in. I relapsed that quickly. It was just like I was watching hard-core porn. My mind replayed every lesbian sex scene with which I had enticed my flesh before, and I found myself thinking thoughts that had not been in my mind for years.

I recall another morning when I was watching a crime show that specialized in sexual assaults. I justified it like I needed to know the signs of criminal activity to be able to identify danger, bad people, and patterns of behavior. Steven would have been about 9 years old, and I remember he came walking in on a very questionable scene. I was ashamed. I paused the show or quickly changed the channel to guard his eyes, but he was quick. "Mommy what are you watching? Why did you change it?" He had 99 questions, and I did not have a valid answer. At that moment, the Holy Spirit convicted me that if something could not be watched by my children, I had no business watching it either. I think of the verse where Jesus tells us that we should come to him like little children. I believe that means to keep a mindset of purity and one of a childlike innocence.

I often ask my Celebrate Recovery moms who struggle with rage or yelling at their small children what they watch on T.V. You would be amazed how many watch these crime shows, talk shows, even shows where a Judge hears family members spew hate and bitterness through the airwaves. You cannot feast on those types of shows and expect to respond to your little ones in love and with compassion.

One of my pastor friends shared with me how he had been enjoying the family-friendly duck show with his daughter. The commercials always seemed to be for a new show about a family of three who moved to a new town where their home was haunted by demons. This show is in its tenth season, and has shown very vivid homosexuality since season one. The commercials have always been intended to entice sexually vulnerable people (with the producer being openly gay). My friend said how horribly uncomfortable it is to be watching a family-friendly show when almost every commercial break had an advertisement for this show with two women always being together. I commented that the same thing happened to me in 2016 when I would be watching super-hero shows with my 16-year-old. There was always this one commercial about a wife who wasn't happy with her marriage, and when the husband got worried about a divorce, she said, "of course not . . . I just want to try some new things . . . let's have a threesome." Then it would zoom in and have second shots of women, and the man, and a prelude to basically group sex. I was utterly shocked. Of course, we never watched the show, but these commercials are on around 7 p.m. when families are sitting down to have family time. What is going on? Formerly, shows like this had to be requested and paid for on channels like Showtime® or HBO. But now it is on Fox.

Another time, my husband and I were looking for the movie, *Les Misérables,* on Netflix. We had seen this movie before and really enjoyed it. I had typed in the first three letters—l-e-s—and before I knew it, dozens of shows on homosexuality, lesbians, and gays appeared on the Netflix screen to choose from. The pictures were provocative and showed half-dressed women together. So my question to you is: "Do you have parental blocks on your Netflix, or can your kids access any show they want?" My boys are now grown. The last one just left the house this past year, so I do not envy the job in front of you. But know this: I do not know of a young boy who could stumble upon a show with two beautiful women half-naked and not take a peek. And to be truthful, had I never encountered those two teenagers kissing in the rain, I do not know that I would have sought out additional lesbian porn. It is not just our young boys we need to be concerned about. This gateway lures our young girls just as easily.

Many times you see someone post on Facebook that they are looking for a new television series to watch. I have noticed multiple women watching shows like the new prison series about women who are locked up. This show has had six seasons. Do you know the amount of people who need to watch a series enough to boost ratings for a new season? My heart is breaking over these teenagers and bored housewives just looking to waste time. Idle time is called the devil's playground for a reason. In this day and age, it is very dangerous. I have had three close Christian friends say how watching this show left them full of regret. They have shared how watching the women in jail and their sexual encounters has opened thoughts and actions that no other show has done before. It is not harmless. Seeds of destruction to everything God stands for are being planted in the hearts and minds of millions of Netflix viewers everywhere.

Are you aware, and do you have Netflix parental controls set on your TV? If you select the link for parental controls in the settings section, you can enter your Netflix account password on the screen. Set your viewing restriction level to the setting you desire. This will require a pin to watch anything over the normal setting.

Today's TV shows all seem to allow a little crude humor, sex before marriage, and a homosexual reference at least once in a season, so why even mention this? What is the solution this day and age with the media? Well it starts by being a present parent.

Deuteronomy 6:6-9 and restated in Deuteronomy 11:19 says, "**Teach them to your children, talking about them when you sit at home, and when you walk along the road, when you lie down, and when you get up"** (NIV). Repetition aids learning; then given examples, good and bad. The key is to water the good and pull up the bad. *If our children are not able to "know the truth," we must call out the Enemy's lies for them until they are able to do it themselves.*

There were several times when others were sowing good seeds into my life. I would send my three boys to church every Sunday on the church bus. This allowed me to sleep or do who knows what, but I just needed the break—or felt I deserved the break. Seems hilarious because my whole life in that season was a break. Without fail, every week, I would find prayer requests from my little boys where they would pray for their mommy to get better. No doubt, I would say every week . . . "Mommy doesn't feel good, could you just leave me alone?" I can tell you it feels horrible to write that! For those three and a half years, I was a pathetic mom. But even God's Word provides comfort in knowing, **"He will make up for the years the locust ate"** (see Joel 2:25). Even if the locusts were mostly my fault. He has made up for all the things the Enemy tried to take from me.

March 3, 2004: I write this knowing that it is not the best thing to do. Your life is your life to do with as you see fit. But my grandfather took me aside one day and told me this story. He told me I could party all week, day-in and day-out. But come Sunday, he said, I had to go to church. If I went out

Saturday till time to go to church, I had to go to church still. He said that one day I would have a family, and I would have to lead that family the right way. My family is out and about, you have to lead your family. That is why I always ask that you go to church with the boys. They only see you partying, they do not see you at church.

Like my grandfather asked me, I now ask you to lead your family. Please go to church with the boys, because, they can be leaders in their family someday. Love always, Father.

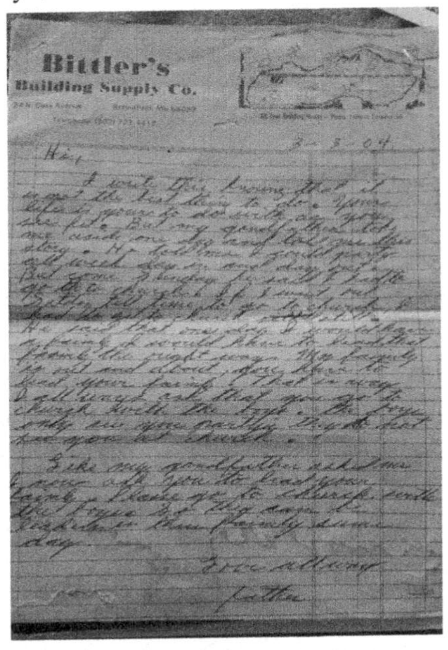

Bittler's
Building Supply Co.

3-3-04

Hi,

Love always
Father

This letter was written two years before I finally got clean, and one year before I would stand before him to boast of my new-found homosexual life. I've shared this letter with hundreds of parents, to tell them . . . I know prayer works. I am living proof, but I also know that sometimes it gets worse before it gets better. This letter sits in my office where I disciple other Celebrate Recovery women. Some are there trying to get their lives back on track. Others may have a child or a husband lost in addiction. This letter is a constant reminder of my father's love for me—

that he loved me too much to turn a blind eye to my rebellious lifestyle.

Please do not stop praying. Do not stop speaking the truth in love. Give those examples and reminders, because: **"God's Word will not return void."** (see Isaiah 55:11).

Just before Tony was about to be released from prison, there was this pull for me to stay the course of destruction. To seek out advice and ask anyone if I should take Tony back would be a "No Way, José!" Mostly because 99 percent of my world was drugs and lies, sex and manipulation. My close friends had selfish hearts which stopped them from being able to encourage the restoration of my marriage. They were paralyzed in their own lives to the fear of the unknown. How could they hope for the best for me?

But God! . . . God was continuing to send people my way to plant seeds of hope and the possibility of a different life. Did Tony's stay in prison really change him? His letters continued to show a strong desire for our marriage to be restored. Earlier in the book, I mentioned "Rob" the pastor who asked us to move to New Orleans to plant the church. Tony and I met Rob during our first marriage while our kids were caught up in the system (wards of the state), just prior to our divorce. Rob would come out and do visits with the older boys. Getting a sense of something different about him, we never knew he was a pastor.

Fast forward to 2005, I worked the Celebrate Recovery steps at his church. He was located just down the street from my mother's house. We talked often, and he never pushed. Because of his knowledge of the fall of my first marriage, and the fact that I knew he had been in contact with Tony, (he even let me use his car one time to go visit Tony in prison) I decided to ask what he thought. Something about the fact that he was always there, patient and kind, and never aggressive or pushy with his religion gave me a sense I could trust him. Now I know it was Holy Spirit. So we met, maybe a month before Tony's parole.

Rob shared that he believed 100 percent that Tony's conversion was true, his faith was strong, and he knew God's desire was for us to be remarried. He then told me he had had visions of him and Anthony sharing a stage, preaching the Word of God together. One year after Tony's release, Rob's church would be the first place Tony would preach a sermon. I have said it before, and I will say it again: **"There are many different voices in this world, and all have meaning"** (see 1 Corinthians 14:10). As parents we must take the time to explain (decipher) those voices to our children. We must be able to know the difference between the people who are speaking into our lives as well.

In 2010, our church was hosting a parenting conference. The author of *Hurt*, (Clark, 2004)[4] Chap Clark was the speaker. I remember how he shared that we have only a short window of time as parents to leave an impression on our children

---

[4] Chap Clark, *Hurt: Inside the World of Today's Teenagers* (Grand Rapids: Baker Academic, 2004).

for the Lord. He believed after much research that Christian education or homeschooling was a must for families in this current culture. The dangers of what public schools were pushing, even indoctrinating, our children into would have huge ramifications. For Anthony and me, this just further solidified that we had made the right decision about enrolling all the boys at Kankakee Trinity Academy. He explained, much like Tony did that day in my mothers' kitchen: "This world will beat our kids up, knock them down, ultimately try to get them to conform or convert to its wicked ways. But as wise, intentional parents, we must remain a step ahead of "the world" by instilling godly principles and values that will last." He shared how in interviewing thousands of 14-24 year olds, many believed they had never been given the tools to be successful adults. He shared with us how thousands of homes and well-meaning parents did not want their children to have to work as hard as they did; they hired someone to cut the grass, clean the house, do the laundry and therefore children were not learning how to live on their own. This is way off topic of media, screen time, and sexual promiscuity . . . but what about the whole picture of helping our children launch into adulthood? Teaching them life skills? I understand wanting to lessen some of the hardships we faced growing up, but some hardships are part of growing up. A large part of the success of our family has been our willingness to be teachable. We know we do not have all the right answers, and we have been blessed to be able to glean from what others have learned. This seminar has significantly shaped how I instruct my teens. He explained that in the Bible there was no Greek word for adolescence. We in America basically came up with that time period (originally 15-18), but now some say the age range is 14-24, where our youth do not have a clue what they want in life. He explained in the times of the Bible, it was a community that helped to raise the children, that a family (mother and father) taught their sons and daughters what it looked like to be an adult, and then one day told them . . . "OK, you're an adult." End of story.

I found it revolutionary that the key to getting our kids out of our basements was in our hands. It looks like intentional parenting. Again, I get it, we are all busy. Understand that the Enemy desires to destroy the family, and we have a choice to make. We must quit being so distracted by laziness and be intentional parents, taking seriously the future of our children. This one seminar had such an impact on my ability as a mother to shape my children's lives. I committed to cultivating an atmosphere for learning a biblical mindset toward life, then launch them into a world where they would not only be light, but make a difference. This night, seeds were watered from when Tony and I sat at my mother's table. I, the mother of these young men, held a key to their future. Are we perfect? No indeed! Have we always gotten it right? Absolutely not! But I know when I stand before God and give an account of how I parented, I did my best to continue to grow and lead by example.

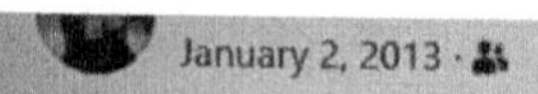

January 2, 2013 ·

As I sat in the movie theatre watching "parental guidance" (a movie about the changing of parent hood and discipline) while a comedy I was forced to think, do I think my parents are doing a bad job? Are there things I would do differently? If so why? And then I think about my parents, although they struggled apart from God in my early years, since I moved from Evansville to St. Anne at age 9 everything was about what God wanted us to do. Even now as I sit, in my livingroom in new Orleans after moving 900 miles because God asked us to. My parents have raised me teaching that Loving others is more important than what I want. Loving JESUS with all my heart is the only thing I can accomplish in this life. So would I do anything differently? No. I would seek God with all my heart, and trust in him to guide me. So this is a thanks to my two wonderful parents for doing that these past 6 years through Christ himself they give the love they have to me.

Facebook post from my son, Miles,
while we lived in New Orleans

Now, in the midst of my addiction, this same son got lost one day after school. He was only about 8 years old and had walked a friend home to get permission for that friend to come play. His friend had to stay home, and somehow Miles had gotten turned around and was completely lost. Without his older brother who normally walked with him everywhere, he began to cry. Meanwhile, oblivious to the dangers that lurk out in the real world, I was at home drinking while I prepared supper. I cannot say for sure how much time had passed before a stranger drove Miles home, but I was never even worried. Miles had been crying so hard his face was beet red. Who knows if I even thanked the guy or saw anything wrong with how

I was parenting. I now know this had to have been one of those moments where Tony was praying fervently for me and our boys. So even though I have the "great memory" that Miles recorded thanks to the Facebook timeline, in my memory is also this parenting failure. There were years where I planted, encouraged, and allowed seeds of death and destruction in my boys. My job now is to work to continue to dig up the bad and create the good, God-honoring teachable moments, to learn from my mistakes, and to share them. I share my mistakes so that prayerfully you won't have to make the same ones.

Multiple times a day, we must make opportunities to share with our children the gospel, the written Word of God, and the truth of the Bible, not what the world promotes. You might ask me what this means. I believe it is our job as parents and grandparents to stop in the middle of these shows and explain to our children why it is wrong. The short and sweet explanation is: *"That is not God's best for you."* I would go one step farther, as I did with the "family-friendly show" my son and I were watching at the beginning of this chapter—Shut the show off! We are the parents. We have the authority over our homes, and it is time we start acting like it. We need parental blocks, and if that is not enough, then maybe your home should not have WIFI. I understand that you might want to have the Internet for yourself. My question is, "What if this is too much for our youth, and it is, in fact, creating more stories like the one earlier in this book?" What if those parents could have done more to stop their son from becoming a pedophile? Please do not wait ten years to find out! What if your unwillingness to monitor the media in and around your home and your children has led to a horrible porn addiction, or homosexual relationships, or worse . . . a rapist and someone caught up in sex trafficking.

I heard a comparison of today's porn access in the home due to parents not being more intentional about what their kids can and cannot view explained like this: "It would be like having all the playboys in a closet that has a lock on the door, but never taking the time to lock it." What sense does that make? You can monitor what your kids see. You control the gateways to their hearts and minds.

Currently, Tony and I have two little ones. We have become foster parents, mostly because of the difference the foster family from Jane Doe's story made in her life. What a gift to be able to help shape a child's life who has experienced trauma and pain. Just last night I was visiting with my sister when I realized my little one had been quiet. As I walked into the living room, he saw me coming. He quickly backed out of what he was watching (on YouTube)--some fight show. Not horrible, but not seeds I plan to water in his little heart. I had just given him access to YouTube that morning to watch worship videos before church. It does not take long for Satan to tempt our children to watch what they have no business watching.

You may be saying "great for you, but I've let my kids do what they want for too many years, and it's too late for my family." It is never too late. God's love story to us is all about broken people wanting to do better. No one is ever without sin. We live in a fallen world, but we can be intentional with how we parent from here on out: **"Though a righteous man falls seven times, he will get up"** (Proverbs 24:16 ESV). Get back up, ask for help, reach out and God will help you to raise your family the way He intended. He has given you His manual. It is time we stop looking to the world and all of these counterfeits. We all make mistakes. But the way you see your mistakes comes down to this: Do you see failure as an event or an identity? A mistake, a failure is what happened, NOT who you are.

In our home, with our little ones, we do not allow headphones. The week that the school passed out computers, when doing a search to check history, we found secular music with violent and very sexual undertones that we do not allow in our home. I recommend not letting kids listen to music through headphones. You should listen to what you want them to listen to. Why do I feel so strongly about the headphones? Our now 20-year-old Fredrick was our first teenager to walk through the unlimited Internet season with us. We have always listened to Christian music in the car or a sermon. He would be in the back with his headphones. I often would intentionally tune in to the lyrics he would be singing, then ask for his phone and look up the song myself. It is accountability. Without throwing him under the bus, I would guess that about five times out of ten, it was something we definitely did not approve. Respectfully, he would change songs, delete songs, and at the risk of losing his phone switch over to Christian rap while in my presence. And for me, that is a minimum of holding our teenagers accountable. We cannot let statements like "it's my phone; I pay for it," allow their music to go unchecked. Or when we notice a child isolating to their room, "it's my room, who cares if my door is always shut." The Enemy operates in secret. We must show our concern. When you stand before God, you will account for your parental actions.

All these forms of media produce entryways into our children's minds. It is that old saying "Idle time is the devil's playground." Without boundaries, that is what is happening. On average, a child between 5 and 16 spends 6.5 hours of screen time a day, with our teen boys over 8 hours. This is a 116 percent increase over the past 25 years.[5] This is numbing our children's hearts and deadening their sense of compassion. Our kids are not getting enough physical activity, nowhere near enough sleep, and the data is all available to prove it. So why are we not listening? Is it wrong if I say we are doing the minimal parenting at best? For our house, intentional parenting around screen time and video games looks like this: Our kids have to do physical playing outside, exercise, or manual labor, like cutting the grass or stacking wood, in addition to reading a book. If they did both of these things for say 30 minutes, they received 30 minutes of game time. For our new little ones, we did summer learning work, and they just had to complete three or four work sheets. We still push the reading, and

---

[5] Site for screen time: printed data.

they normally do not have to be told to go play, but that is still and will always be a must. Physical activity is so important. Currently, 77 percent of kids do not get enough physical activity, and the average kid plays outside for only four hours a week. This is destructive behavior. Being connected to a screen most of your waking hours is unhealthy.

Regarding the court case, the key question I kept asking myself was: "Could this man's parents have known his struggles? Did he show signs of being a sexual deviant? Are we failing our children with free access to the Internet, letting them watch evening T.V. without concern of the content they are able to see?" I ask this because what is PG13 now would have been rated R ten or fifteen years ago. Parents, we cannot fall asleep at the wheel on this one. The shows that are available on Netflix and Hulu are filled with nudity, sex with multiple partners, and homosexuality. Our children are not ready to witness these things. It is causing an increase in porn addiction and a decrease in their sensitivity and compassion. The new reality is that here in America sex trafficking does exist. There are predators on the other side of the computer screen, and our kids are too trusting. All the dangers have become magnified over the past ten years. They all have to do with Media, the Internet, lack of supervision, and maybe even ignorance on the parents' part. There are scriptures that depict Satan as the "**god of this world**" (2 Corinthians 4:4 ESV), and described him "**as the prince of the power of the air**" (Ephesians 2:2 NKJV). In preparation for this book, the Holy Spirit has revealed many things to me. One of the key messages behind this book you are holding is that Satan is using media; i.e., cell phones, Facebook, Internet, Netflix, streaming, scrolling, music, movies, cable television, video games. Any form of media that can travel through the "airwaves" can be used by the Enemy. I am coming to expose his ways!

My prayer is that you have googled my book to either help a loved one you know struggling with sexual sin, same-sex attraction, or you are being proactive. Whatever your reason for picking up this book, I know there is real freedom. Now, we need to explore some of the most common half-truths the Enemy is using in the media.

Chapter 8

Biblical Truths Satan Twists

> People do not drift toward holiness; they drift toward compromise and call it tolerance. They drift toward disobedience and call it freedom.
>
> —D.A. Carson

I gave this chapter its title loosely, because in researching for this book, and just in everyday life, it is so apparent how the Enemy's agenda focuses on breaking up the biblical family. Satan has no greater agenda than to attempt to desecrate what God creates. Most people who try to discuss biblical marriage are on the two extremes. We have some from the LBGTQ community screaming "hate crimes" at Christians who are willing to stick up for their traditional values. They have called us intolerant. However, it really seems homosexuals are the ones who are intolerant of Christians. But, let us not forget the other drastic side of this argument—some Christians come in with "Bibles blazing," quoting Scripture, and screaming about hell. While the Scriptures are a valid point, you cannot be mean to people to get them to see your side. This topic can seem to bring out the worst in many Christians. My goal is to discuss truth from the middle.

One thing you should consider when sharing "truth" with people—Who is your audience? Are they Christians who can walk through the Scriptures to understand your case? Or, are they so against God that quoting the Bible is not even an option? This is where the screaming matches are birthed.

I have 10 questions or statements that seem to be at the top of the debate between LGBTQ and Christians. Many of these slightly distorted truths were part of my thought process in justifying my past sexual choices.

(1) Let's talk truth.

What is truth vs. post truth?

John 8:32 says, **"You will know the truth, and the truth will set you free"** (ESV).

Here is an excerpt from Webster's American 1828 Dictionary of the English Language, Publisher's Preface:

> Language is an expression of ideas, and as ideas change over time, words take on new meanings. Hence, Noah Webster's 1828 publication, *An American Dictionary of the English Language*, is a work of great importance to modern readers who care

> about traditional values. The founding documents of the United States of America are contemporary with this 1828 dictionary, as are many other important books and documents of that time. The 1828 dictionary defines the language of these materials in the context of their era and thus becomes a valuable reference tool to enhance understanding. In addition, Noah Webster based his work extensively on the King James Version of the Bible, so that not only the words but also the values of the early nineteenth century are reflected in the definitions. As Webster wrote, "In my view, the Christian religion is the most important and one of the first things in which all children, under a free government ought to be instructed . . . No truth is more evident to my mind than that the Christian religion must be the basis of any government intended to secure the rights and privileges of a free people.

Oxford Languages defines post-truth as: "relating to or denoting circumstances in which objective facts are less influential in shaping public opinion that appeals to emotion and personal belief."[1] Post-truth was Oxford's "word of the year" in 2016.

Dictonary.com defines post-truth as: "Relating to or existing in an environment in which facts are viewed as irrelevant, or less important than personal beliefs and opinions, and emotional appeals are used to influence public opinion."

---

[1]*Oxford English Dictionary,* (n.d.). http://www.oed.com/view/Entry/156942#eid1211161030.

Is this not the meaning behind (2 Timothy 4:2-5)?

> **Proclaim the message; persist in it whether convenient or not rebuke, correct, and encourage with great patience and teaching. For the time will come when they will not tolerate sound doctrine, but according to their own desires, will multiply teachers for themselves because they have an itch to hear something new. They will turn away from hearing the truth and will turn aside to myths. But as for you, be serious about everything, endure hardship, do the work of an evangelist, fulfill your ministry (HCSB).**

The gospel is meant to change the sinner, not the sinner to change the gospel to suit their sin. We see this in the church, the divide that allows homosexuals to have positions in the pulpit. ***Let me clarify this. The church is the place for the broken, but the church cannot have unrepentant sin in a leadership role.***

John says, **"Light exposes dark, whoever lives by the truth comes into the light"** (see 3:21). One of my favorite quotes from my pastor, Dr. Michael Knight, is: "You can't obey what you don't know." If you do not know God's Word, His plan for your life, His boundaries, you cannot possibly know how to make things work.

I am not trying to be intolerant of other people's beliefs; I really am not. But Jesus said, **"I am the way, the truth, and the life. No one comes to the Father except through Me"** (John 14:6 NKJV). And I believe Jesus.

I did not write this book to demand you see things my way based on my feelings. I want to share the truth based on the never-changing Word of God. Hebrews 13:8 tells us, **"Jesus Christ is the same yesterday, today, and forever"** (NKJV).

Now, more than ever, we need truth found in God's Word, not people's views, not people's opinions, and not people's theories! Absolute Truth

One of my favorite preachers (and there are probably 20 I watch and listen to weekly), *is Michael Todd. His sermon series "Relationship Goals" came out in 2017, and that is when I first started listening to him. This year, 2020, he did a series called "Relationship Goals Reloaded,"* and released his book *Relationship Goals,* and it is EXCELLENT! I listened to it the first day it was available on audio, and literally . . . many of the concepts I discuss here, he openly discusses in his book. For a pastor to be transparent about sexual sin is nothing short of refreshing and so needed in this day and age. He often talks about Psalms 119. To remain pure, you must hide yourself in the Word of God. He calls it his "go-to." Psalm 119 is a list of statutes, ways, commands, precepts, laws, or Word of the Lord. It is a repetition of right and wrong. It is where we find God's truth. These important principles are found in God's Word. Now, more than ever, we need truth, not people's views, opinions, or theories.

John 17:17 says, **"Sanctify them by the truth; Your Word is truth"** (HCSB).

When we know truth that is founded in God's Word, we are able to stand firm, knowing beyond a shadow of a doubt what is fact. God will never tell you to do something that contradicts His Word. It does not matter if you "feel" strongly like you have God's approval. His approval lines up with His Word—the Holy Scriptures.

We find this "gray" area when we stop seeing things as one of two sides. It is called categorical thinking. We hold fast to the bigger picture that God creates and Satan corrupts. In a sermon the other day by Eric Gilbert from 3Trees Church, he shared this topic of categorical thinking and compared it to our dualistic surroundings. He explained how we have holiness, and the Enemy creates sin; and how we have made our own category to be a "lifestyle choice." This takes the focus off us trying to be holy to almost justifying our sin or wrong behavior. And this is the gray area with truth. This is the whole premise for my book. Feelings are not facts. Therefore, how you feel cannot be what determines truth.

(2) If God is love, shouldn't I just love everyone?

As Christians, love should be the motivational factor, with restoration as the end game for pointing out sin!

I will not demand you believe what I believe. That is not love. However, it is unloving to not tell the truth, not post true feelings, but biblical facts.

1 Corinthians 13:4-8 (HCSB):	Translations quoted to the side are for a fuller understanding of these scriptures.
v. 4: **"Love is patient, Love is kind."**	Love does not envy, is not boastful, is not conceited.
	ESV: **Not arrogant or rude.**
v. 5: **"Does not act improperly."**	MSG: **Doesn't force itself on others.**
	NLT: **Does not demand its own way.**
"Is not selfish."	Is not provoked. And does not keep a record of wrongs.
v. 6: **"Love finds no joy in unrighteousness."**	NIV: **Does not delight in evil.**
	ESV: **Does not rejoice in wrongdoing.**
"But rejoices in truth."	
v. 7: **"Love bears all things."**	NIV: **Always protects**
"Believes all things."	Trusts
"Hopes all things."	Hopes
"Endures all things."	Perseveres
v. 8: **"Love never ends."**	

Love does not tolerate sin, does not look the other way, or sweep it under the rug. Love does not smile and say, "to each his own." Love also does not belittle, mock, or condemn others. Love does not rejoice at wrongdoing, but rejoices with the truth.

When I say I love you, I cannot impose my way on you. I cannot insist that you see things my way. But, love does not delight in evil. I cannot celebrate your acts of rebellion toward God's boundaries. When I say that love rejoices in truth, that is a truth I must communicate in love. Whether someone accepts that truth is between them and God, but to not tell someone the end result of their lifestyle choices is really not love.

This is the foundation for what I know.

"God is love."	ESV: 1 John 4:8
Jesus has commanded: "Love your neighbor as yourself."	NIV: Mark 12:31
Jesus has told us to go into all the world and share the gospel.	NIV: Mark 16:14 We are not to add this part or leave out that part; all parts are the good news—the whole gospel.
God is not a liar and cannot contradict Himself.	Numbers 23:19: Thus, we cannot leave out parts about sexuality because we are concerned we may offend someone.

Loving people means telling them hard truths about lifestyle choices they are making, even if we know at that time it may not be received well.

A sermon series, "Beauty and the Beast," by Pastor Jon Hill at First Church DeMotte from three years ago had a great deal of information I have used. He made a very valid argument about the way we approach alcoholics and drug addicts versus the way we approach those trapped in a homosexual lifestyle. Is it because we know the end result for an addict is death or prison? We would never throw a parade and celebrate someone who is a full-blown alcoholic with liver complications due to drinking every day. When we noticed them shaking because of withdrawals, we would not encourage them to try a different brand of liquor like the end result will not be the same. I remember my broken heart from a relationship out of marriage that was destined to not succeed outside of God's perfect plan, and how the coworker offered up homosexuality as if a different form of sexual deviancy would give me a better result to my heartache. Do you know the definition of insanity according to Albert Einstein? Doing the same thing over and over, expecting a different result. We use this example in Celebrate Recovery for what happens when not changing past dangerous behaviors.

A study group[2] was interviewed consisting of 2.4 million heterosexual youth and 113,468 LGBT

---

[2] LGBT, Suicide Stats for Teens, May 6, 2019.

A study in 2018 finds LGBT teenagers are three times more likely to attempt suicide.

youth all ranging in ages from 12 to 20. These are the results: LGBT youth were 3.5 times more likely to attempt suicide, with gay and lesbian youth being 3.71 times higher, and bisexual youth at 3.69 times more likely to attempt suicide than teens who identify as heterosexual. Why are we celebrating something that is obviously causing so much pain and torment? Why then, when we have the chance to minister to someone in sexual bondage are we so scared to talk about purity, abstaining, wrong sexual thought patterns, and building a relationship with Christ? The only place where true freedom from everything can be found is Christ, and Christ alone. John 8:36 says, **"Therefore, if the Son sets you free, you really will be free" (HCSB).**

(3) Doesn't God want to give me the desires of my heart?

It seems to me that the world, and even some Christians, have the desires of their hearts and desires of their flesh mixed up.

Psalm 37:4 states, **"Delight yourself in the LORD, and he will give you the desires of your heart" (ESV).** The *Contemporary English Version* states: **"Do what the LORD wants, and he will give you your heart's desire" (CEV).** And the *Good News Translation* says, **"Seek your happiness in the LORD, and he will give you your heart's desire" (GNT).**

When I am walking with God, when I am doing the Lord's will for my life and finding my happiness in the Lord, then yes my spirit's motives will line up with God's will for my life. The end result is that I will have heavenly desires He will fulfill here on earth.

Earlier, I quoted, "You steer where you stare," as something I share on a regular basis. In researching this book, I began to stare at and meditate on things I had no business looking at in my flesh--my flesh that I try to die to daily because (Romans 8:13) tells us: "**For if you live according to the flesh, you are going to die. But if by the Spirit you put to death the deeds of the body (flesh), you will live"**(ESV). In this sinful flesh, I can take a double take at a beautiful man or woman. That is the lust of the flesh. That is my sinful nature trying to come back to life. When sharing how easy it is to get caught up again in watching things God has convicted my heart not to watch . . . it goes back to what Paul says in Romans 7:15-20:

> **I do not understand what I do. For what I want to do I do not do, but what I hate I do. And if I do what I do not want to do, I agree that the law is good. As it is, it is no longer I myself who do it, but it is sin living in me. For I know that good itself does not dwell in me, that is, in my sinful nature. For I have the desire to do what is good, but I cannot carry it out. For I do not do the good I want to do, but the evil I do not want to do— this I keep on doing. Now if I do what I do not want to do, it is no longer I who do it, but it is sin living in me that does it"** (NIV).

Twelve years clean, four years free from perversion of mind, I found myself having sexual thoughts and fantasies that were not my own, that were not welcome, that even at this moment disgust me for how quickly we can fall back into temptation. Satan would cause me to feel unqualified to write a book on biblical marriage or sexually pure living when I myself would have such wicked thoughts and knowing that it is not God's best for me. We all make mistakes, but the way you see your mistakes comes down to this: Do you see failure as an event or an identity? Just because in my flesh I am weak and I watched things I regret does not by any means make me a failure. My identity is not found in mistakes that Satan wants to hammer into my heart. My identity comes from who my Creator says I am—**"a new creature in Christ"** (see 2 Corinthians 5:17). And that is found in the truth of God's Word. Proverbs 24:16 tells me, **"Though a righteous man falls seven times, he will get up"** (HCSB). It is never too late to get back up.

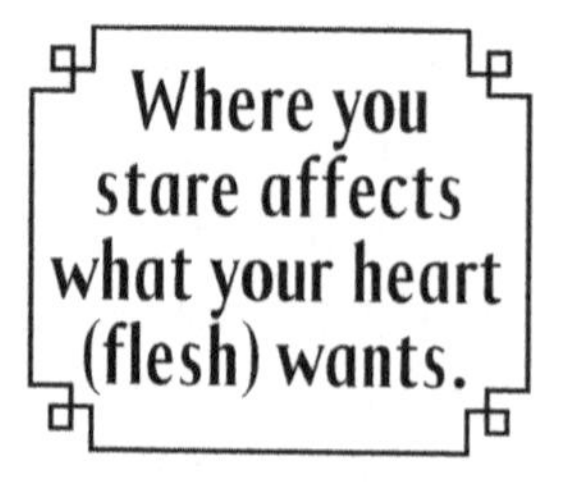

> **Being tempted does not mean I am not saved. It just means I am human.**

Back to steering where you stare. It was when David "stared" at Bathsheba, he began to desire something that was not God's best for him. All sin action has to begin with sin thought. What are we staring at? What are we meditating on in our minds? When Lot was looking out over Sodom and Gomorrah, when he pitched his tent and looked in that direction, he began to "stare" and eventually went from worshiping God at an altar with his Uncle Abram to running back to captivity in one of the most well-known wicked places of all the Bible.

In making these confessions with my dear friends who are helping me write this book, I said, "I hate that there is that side of my flesh that is so sinful." Know this: I love my husband. Words do not even begin to explain the one million reasons I love him. I love serving in ministry beside Tony, watching him pray for men at the altar, glancing over and seeing his hands lifted in worship, feeling his embrace as he holds me close and prays in the Spirit over me, watching him with our grandchildren, and now as he so peacefully teaches our new little ones (the foster kids). That is a level of love that until you get to experience chasing after God with the person God destined you to be with as a helpmate, you cannot even fathom it. So yes, my flesh has desires to which I must die DAILY. (But my heart desires, and wants to live a life pleasing to Him). I could not be more attracted to my husband. He is everything to me. And our love just continues to grow deeper with each year that passes and each new season that begins. God knew what he was doing when he placed a love inside Tony's heart for me. He knew Tony could be trusted to nurture, provide, protect, and pray for and with me, and lead and guide, and passionately love me. I get all this from my marriage. Yes, God has in fact given me **"the desires of my heart"** (see Psalm 37:4).

Jackie Hill Perry gives an excellent example of the difference between the spirit woman and dying to her flesh. In the book, *Gay Girl, Good God,* Jackie talks about the process of becoming the woman God created her to be. How at the onset of her day, as she gets dressed every morning, she offers up a sacrifice of who she was for who God has called her to be. She stated it as dying to the old Jackie who would have worn men's boxers and walking out who God created her to be as a woman by putting on ladies panties (author paraphrased).[3] I found it fascinating how she shared that even the act of putting on her undergarments she felt was a surrender. A daily discipline of keeping who she used to be, nailed to the cross. She said the very act of wearing ladies garments caused her to walk differently, more femininely as God had always intended.

(4) It is all the same end result, right?

This was the statement made to me when I was 20. This could not be further from the truth. Sex does have a gratification side to it; however, in Genesis 1:27-28, God's intention is made clear: **"So God created man in His own image; He created him in the image of God; He created them male and female. God blessed them, and God said to them, "Be fruitful, multiply, fill the earth, and subdue it"** (HCSB).

---

[3] Jackie Hill Perry, *Gay Girl, Good God* (Nashville: B&H Books, 2018).

God's directive is very clear with "the end result" being the procreation of life—one man, and one woman. Filling the earth cannot be done with two people of the same sex. That is in no way what God intended.

Now, let me take you for a walk to find this world's interpretation of "the same end result." I went to Jane Doe's mother's final court date. She was given a lesser charge, ended up on probation, and lost custody of her child. As she was meeting with her probation officer for the first time, we went to get a burger afterwards. In this restaurant, she saw a man who had abused her daughter. He testified against the father to avoid charges after being found incompetent to stand trial. But the truth of the matter is that he paid the father to have sexual contact with the 12-year-old girl. She was horribly confused. She told me. "I don't get it. He's gay. He is only attracted to men. I know my daughter didn't lie. If she said it happened, it happened. But I would never have seen him as a threat because he had made the comment freely how he was only into men." I shared with her that sin, sexual sin, only takes you darker and darker, and that the end result becomes what a person seeks, and it is driven by their flesh. In a terribly fallen world, the desires of the flesh rule. Where Satan is the god (little g) of this world, yes, a person could say for the physical side, it is all the same end result—sexual fulfillment. But same end result for whom? No kid says, "Please force me to have sex with 30 men a day." No women are really experiencing a climax in the porn industry with every scene portraying enjoyment. In researching for this book, I found a podcast called: "The Van Maren Show" from the frontlines of the culture war. Presented by LifeSite, I have listened to dozens of episodes on pornography and the sex industry. Topics range from "Porn Changes Your Brain, but You Can Change It Back," to "The Truth About Pornography With Former Porn Actress, Jessica Neely." She shared how they were told that if they didn't act like they are having a good time, they would be done, fired, and never go to work again. The fact is that porn is darker and darker than ever before. More children are being sold and abused. She shared that because of the Internet and such a strong presence to soft porn readily available that the porn industry has become unbearable. They have to keep their customers coming back with more and more creative, violent, and deviant scenes than you could imagine. After listening to her testimony, I cried and just thanked God that He kept me from making connections and getting caught up in that lifestyle. The old Nikki . . . Chapter 3 Nikki . . thought she was going to be the female version of Hugh Heffner and Jenna Jameson mixed. Boy was I deceived. Thank you, Jesus, for protecting me from myself. My research proved my own personal experience. Pornography serves as the gateway for many and leads to sexual dysfunction. Pornography is rapidly increasing and its viewers are getting younger. This book is just the tip on an iceberg I can't fathom trying to uncover more. There is a much darker world out there. I am not going to get into trafficking and sexual abuse of children. Not in this book anyway.

But, the darkness needs to be exposed. I just know that this young girl's story sparked me to share mine.

There is God's way, and this world's way. Any sexual pleasure is not the same end result. I said before, only God knows the true heart of a man, and where they will end up—heaven versus hell. But if there is even a possibility that this could alter your eternity, that is one end result I am begging you to consider. It is not worth the chance. Proverbs 14:12 says, **"There is a way that seems right to a man, but its end is the way to death"** (HCSB).

(5) I can't change, or was I born this way?

Let me say if that were the truth, then I would still have a needle sticking out of my arm.

> "Just because a guy struggles with same-sex desire does not mean God made him gay, any more than a guy struggling with anger means God made him a murderer. You have a choice about what you do with every temptation."
>
> —Ray Comfort

The problem with the slogan, "I can't help it; I was born that way" is that the Bible clearly states that we are given our identity at birth. Male or female is a natural part of that identity. Anything after that is a choice. So if the statement, "I can't help it; I was born this way" were true, then this would be true for everyone who has made the choices that landed them in jail or prison. But that's the key: The choices they made landed them in prison. James 1:14,15 tells us: **"But each one is tempted when he is dragged away, enticed and baited [to commit sin] by his own [worldly] desire (lust, passion). Then when the illicit desire has conceived, it gives birth to sin; and when sin has run its course, it gives birth to death** (AMP).

Everything after birth becomes a choice. We have a choice to go to school, get an education and be a functioning part of society. Or, we can be a dropout, put forth minimal effort, and be a leech on society, or live in your parents' basement. It is the same with people who choose to take God's Word for what it is—truth. They set themselves apart trying their very best by the help of Jesus and the Holy Spirit to live the way God intended us to live—God's best plan for us. I will never claim to have it all together, or to be perfect. I am progressing, learning, still teachable, still moving toward the goal. Philippians 3:14 says, **"I pursue as my goal the prize promised by God's heavenly call in Christ Jesus** (HCSB).

And then there are those who are lost souls, searching and seeking for that missing piece. When it comes to our children, this book's intention is to identify the threat so you as the parent know how to protect your child from seeds of darkness being planted by the lies of the Enemy. Folks it is as simple as that: "God's way or the Enemy's way." There are people on this earth representing one side or the other. If you have picked up this book because you (or someone you love) have found yourself empty, broken, and wanting more . . . there is more. I have been right where you are, sick and tired of being sick and tired. I am telling you that a relationship with Jesus is the only answer that lasts, being connected daily to the Living Vine.

John writes, **"Abide in Me, and I in you. As the branch cannot bear fruit by itself unless it abides in the vine, neither can you unless you abide in Me"** (John 15:4 ESV).

I would like to challenge you that the multiple times Jesus commands us to abide or remain in the vine are because there are multiple ways for us to abide. Sunday morning church services (fellowship/community) is not the only way believers abide. We pray, fast, study, serve, seek, meditate, give, submit, disciple, simplify, and worship. I will dive deeper into these in the last chapter.

We must transform our minds. We were intentional to seek out destructive behaviors for the many years we were in bondage. So now we must be intentional to get rid of those layers of garbage, of filth. The Bible tells us in Philippians 4:8: **"Finally, brothers and sisters, whatever is true, whatever is noble, whatever is right, whatever is pure, whatever is lovely, whatever is admirable—if anything is excellent or praiseworthy—think about such things"** (NIV).

That means if you struggle with lust, you can't watch the shows on T.V. that show affairs, and steamy scenes. If your marriage is having problems, maybe reading racy romance novels is not helping matters. My book is titled after a series I know is contrary to how God wants your relationship to be.

You have a choice about what you do with every temptation. God reminds us that **"Sin is crouching at your door; it desires to have you, but you must rule over it"** (Genesis 4:7 NIV). Are you having a problem walking away from whatever the label is, "I can't help it; I was born this way?" Perhaps you have heard the following excuses:

"I'm not a morning person."

"I'm not a hard worker like my sister."

"I'm not a leader like Tommy."

"I'm just always going to make minimum wage."

"I'm always going to struggle with this drinking problem."

"It is the family curse, and it will always be this way."

"I'm just big boned; I'll never be thin."

"We have always been poor; that's just the cards I was dealt."

"Other people have happy marriages; I'm ok just getting along."

"I've never really wanted to get married, because it's never worked out for anyone else."

"Once a drug addict always a drug addict."

Know this: THESE ARE LIES FROM THE DEVIL, and often it just seems normal to say them. Proverbs 6:2 says, **"You are snared by the words of your mouth"** (ESV).

When we say, "I can't help how I am; God created me this way; this is who I am," we are in fact calling God a liar. Yes, we all have certain tendencies to sin. We all have areas that we need to submit to God. As a born-again Christian, we know that process to be called sanctification. Knowing that our words have power, what we say about ourselves bears weight on the process of finding freedom.

We are faced with a culture screaming at Christians as "haters" any time they speak up for biblical values. Our children are beginning to question their gender identities. We have to speak up in love.

It was legal to kill Jews during WW2. It was legal to own black people from 1776 until 1865 here in the USA. And being born a Jew, or African American is something a person cannot change. Legal often is framed by what society deems socially acceptable. None of these things are right even though they are legal. For me as a Christian, I go back to: What is truth? Where is my moral compass? What am I saying about this situation? I have many women I mentor through Celebrate Recovery who struggle with sexual sin. Their addiction to drugs was against the law, but sex with multiple partners is not illegal. Sex outside of marriage is not illegal so they do not hold these stronger convictions yet. This again is why we must be connected to the vine and fill our hearts and minds with the truth of God's Word, not this wicked world's standards.

Just because it is legal does not make it right by God's standards.

(6) Doesn't God want me to be happy?

It all comes back to the difference between our flesh and our spirit man. Our definition of happy changes when our focus changes from being self-focused (selfish), to being Christ-centered.

First Peter 1:14-16 says, **"So you must live as God's obedient children. Don't slip back into your old ways of living to satisfy your own desires. You didn't know any better then. But now you must be holy in everything you do, just as God who chose you is holy. For the Scriptures say, you must be holy because I am holy"** (NLT).

Living as a Christian does not mean I have it all together, and I am perfect or without sin. It means I work on my relationship with Christ and out of that flows a closeness with Him that causes me to hate the sin—to hate anything that would separate me from God the Father.

God sets boundaries to keep us safe. In *Steven Furtick's "Meant to Be"*[4] series, he shared the example of fire. A fire kept in the parameters of a fireplace will provide heat to keep your home warm. But that same fire started outside a fireplace, like in the middle of your living room floor, would burn your house down. This is what we are finding with God's boundaries for sex within the confines of marriage. Sex just anyway can lead to bondage, depression, divorce, rape, and a many other things.

Let me put it this way. We let our dog run from the front door to her leash outside. She has one on the side of the house and one out front. About a week ago, when I let her out the side, she caught a glimpse of a deer and ran into the woods behind

---

[4] Steven Furtick, "Meant to Be" Series, YouTube.

our house. So, now she has to be walked on a leash to the outside tether. It is a boundary so she does not get beaten to death by a deer. (I have watched the videos; it happens, folks.)

Just three or four days ago, I let her off the tether out front (to which she has always—100 percent of the time—run to our front door). But this day she bolted across the busy highway to the neighbor's dog. Guess what my husband and I did that afternoon? We bought a $300 shock collar and invisible fence, because our dog needs additional boundaries. If we let her run and do what she wants, she could be killed by an animal or a car. Boundaries do not mean we do not love our dog; we want her to be happy. They mean we want her to live.

In our walk with God, there comes a place where we want to enjoy life here on earth, instead of just living in fear of going to hell. The Holy Spirit leads you into a life of sanctification and holiness that matures you past that place of "just getting into heaven." As we grow in our walk with God, we get to a place where we lead our hearts instead of being led by our emotions or looking for that "happy" feeling. Paul tells us in (Philippians 4:11) **"I don't say this out of need, for I have learned to be content in whatever circumstances I am"** (HCSB).

(7) Double lie ... Christians see homosexuality worse than other sexual sin, and the LGBTQ community justifies their action according to scriptures that condemn tattoos etc.

Sin is sin is sin. At the foot of the cross it is all filthy rags. Gossip may be harder for people to judge because you do not "see it" like you see two men holding hands. Homosexual relationships tend to be a little more "in your face" than your traditional relationships. Nowadays just because a guy and girl live together and go to church together many times no one knows whether they are married or not. Sexual sin is sexual sin. All sex outside of biblical marriage is still sin.

When the LGBTQ or others who cast blame try to throw tattoo's at a believer . . . we must remember, its a refining (sanctification process) for all. The danger is knowing something is sin, and living in unrepentant acts of disobedience towards God.

(8) Less Abuse in a homosexual relationship.

Lesbian relationships have a higher abuse rate than any other relationships.

Until I watched that sermon series "Beauty and the Beast," I had no idea that there was so much domestic abuse in homosexual relationships. Honestly, it is the No. 1 lie I fell for. A woman will never be able to overpower you like my experience with Tony before he went to prison. According to the CDC and Department of Justice,[5] 90 percent of lesbian women surveyed had suffered from acts of verbal aggression, and in another study, numbers as high as 46 percent of lesbian women had been with a violent partner. Bisexual women have

---

[5] Department of Justice Statistics.

the highest numbers of abuse by a partner at 75 percent; with gay men at 40 percent; and bi-sexual men at 47 percent. To understand the weight of the difference, in the same study straight women had experienced 43 percent (only 3 percent less, yet 32 percent less than bi-sexual women). And the men's numbers are significantly less for heterosexuals with just 21 percent (19 percent and 26 percent over all LESS). According to the Bureau of Justice Statistics (U.S. Department of Justice), married women in conventional families experience the lowest rate of violence compared with women in other types of relationships. Gay men account for 28-30 percent of the domestic abuse that takes place. If you add those numbers up, that indicates three times the abuse of heterosexual relationships. It is the highest level of abuse in any sector throughout society. These statistics further validate Question 2, that if you love someone, and you know that these relationships end in violence, why would we not speak up in love?

(9) Can you be gay and a Christian?

I am a Christian. Not a recovering drug addict Christian, not a nagging wife Christian, not an overprotective mom Christian, and not a bisexual Christian. I am just a Christian. The old me, my sin nature, has been crucified on the cross with Christ. Are there days when certain struggles come out more than before? Yes. But that is why in my weakness, through Christ I find strength. Because if I could do it on my own, I would forget I need Jesus. In 2 Corinthians 12:10, Paul tells us, **"Therefore,**

I take pleasure in infirmities, in reproaches, in needs, in persecutions, in distresses for Christ's sake. For when I am weak, then I am strong" (NKJV). This verse to me that when I have struggles, I keep humble and remember I need Jesus.

I think the real reason people want to ask this question is to trip up a Christian much like the Pharisees tried to trip up Jesus. I do not think we can claim to be connected to the vine, in relationship with Jesus, and not be actively working to shed our sin nature. However, each man's walk with Christ is between that individual and God. Each man will give his own account of the life he has lived. I do not personally think, according to my understanding of the lordship of Jesus Christ, that people are living their best Christian lives with unrepentant sin. Living with a same-sex partner, multiple partners, unmarried according to biblical marriage . . . all those things are active sin which appears to be unrepentant. But, I cannot assume to know someone's heart.

It is not a gay to straight thing; it is a lost to saved thing.

Please also know this. **It is not a gay to straight thing; it is a lost to saved thing.** For some it may look like a life of celibacy or abstaining from relationships. My story is extremely unique having Tony come get me the way he did.

I have heard it said this way: "When you get married, every attractive person in the world does not instantly become ugly." To me, I think Satan kept me bound for so long, just because I wanted the temptations to be gone when I made the commitment to follow Jesus. And sometimes, that is just not the way things work. Temptation just proves we are human, not that we really are not saved. Temptations are going to come. It is what we do with those thoughts that matters, and if we allow them to become actions, they will give birth to sin.

(10) Feelings are not facts.

In everything we do, we must lead our hearts. Jeremiah 17:9 says, **"The human heart is the most deceitful of all things, and desperately wicked. Who really knows how bad it is?"**(NLT).

What I want people to do is think outside their box. I have experienced that most people who are living in a sexually deviant lifestyle of any kind are being driven mostly by their feelings and interpretations of past experiences. I believe this is true for a vast majority of the LGBTG community.

Feelings can change. Feelings have no way to keep us set on a moral path where there is a right and a wrong. Our actions flow from our hearts. We know that **"out of the abundance of the heart the mouth speaks"** (Luke 6:45 NKJV). And we know that we are to **"keep [our] heart with all vigilance, for from it flow the springs of life"** (Proverbs 4:23 NRSV). So at the core, we have a wicked heart. When we let our feelings lead us from our heart, we can do things that are 100 percent wrong but seem to feel so right.

We must hate the sin, not the sinner. The bottom line is we will all stand before God one day and give an account for the life that we have lived. I cannot just stand by while there are people who want help. Hurting people need help. I know the answers and will not remain silent anymore.

In all situations in life, we must lead our hearts. I tell moms every day, "Feelings are not facts." Just because I feel a certain way does not mean that's truth. I may not feel like going to work, but the Bible says, **"If you don't work, you don't eat"** (2 Thessalonians 3:10 CEV). So, I get up and go to work. I lead my heart.

I may not feel like going to church every Sunday, but the Bible says, **"Let us not neglect meeting together, as some people do, but encourage one another . . . Not forsaking our assembly"** Hebrews 10:25 NLT).

I may not feel like submitting to my husband, but the Bible says in (Ephesians 5:22) **"Wives, submit yourselves to your own husbands as to the Lord"** (NKJV).

And so even when my flesh and my heart are encouraging me to not submit to my husband, like I said earlier . . . I look up to heaven and smile because God sees my heart. I want to please God, and I silently ask for help submitting because above all else, I want to please God.

I may not feel like listening to a podcast, sermon, or worship music, but one of the HUGEST lessons Tony and I have learned is found in (Matthew 12:43-45):

> **When an impure spirit comes out of a person, it goes through dry arid places seeking rest, and does not find it. Then it says, I will return to the house I**

> **left. When it arrives, it finds the house unoccupied, swept clean and put in order. Then it goes and takes with it seven other spirits more wicked than itself, and they go in and live there. And the final condition of that person is worse than the first** (NIV).

So even when I do not feel like "filling my house" with teachings, the Word of God, or worship music . . . I know what happens when I leave my house empty. RELAPSE. And this goes for anything. That impure spirit you may be working on can be drugs or sex, or it may just be pride, or gossiping. But if you do not fill your house with knowledge and the truth of God's Word on a regular basis . . . it is coming back with seven other spirits and you will not stand a chance.

So, I do not choose feelings over facts. My heart, my flesh, my feelings will lead me to destruction.

Chapter 9

My Help Comes From the Lord

Don't you see how wonderfully kind, tolerant, and patient God is with you? Does this mean nothing to you? Can't you see that his kindness is intended to turn you from your sin?
(Romans 2:4 NLT).

For it is the goodness and kindness of God that leads men to repentance!

In 2006, when Tony showed up at my doorstep and asked to come in to talk, I honestly was shocked. Why would he want me when I was sure he heard what kind of lifestyle I had been living? I could not fathom why he would want to come talk to me, and it was even harder for me to understand his desire to restore our marriage. I was a bitter, angry, woman when I opened that door. It was definitely a God moment that took place that day, because where hatred and pain had resided in my heart those years he was in prison, it was like . . . God made those emotions shrink so small, it allowed me to remember the man I fell in love with. I often tell people that is the day that God's forgiveness washed over me. I invited him in, and we sat down at the kitchen table. Of course, I shared earlier in the book, how this encounter with the love of Christ through my husband's actions changed me forever. That day I had my very own Damascus Road experience where the scales fell off my eyes. Until that day, I had never felt the presence and love of God so strongly. I witnessed a change in Tony, and I wanted what Tony had. Now I was ready to listen to all the things he had tried to share with me before. Tony needed to get back to the Salvation Army in Kankakee which was four hours and 30 minutes north of Evansville. He asked me if I would drive him back so we could talk some more. I agreed. I have always loved Tony. Tony before Jesus was really the best man I knew. He was a great guy, a hardworking, loving father, and (in the beginning of our first marriage) an attentive husband. This new and improved Tony sounded amazing. He admitted his place in the whole mess and said he wanted to start over. He wanted never to talk about the past (his or mine) because nothing good could come from that. He explained his reasoning was because according to Paul, when we are born again, we are a new creation, one that has never even been seen before. By dredging up the past, the only thing that would do is cause pain and give the Enemy a way to cause division.

We drove, he talked, and I listened. He was so patient with me, explaining things that God had shown him, things we did wrong, and things we would have to do if we were going to get back together. Tony made it very clear, that God had revealed areas in our lives that we had to protect and had to be committed to. Church was a must, only Christian music and TV, as well as cut most of our family out . . . he meant we would still see them on holidays, but hanging out would not happen again. No contact whatsoever with any of our old friends or anyone drug related. Basic 101 of AA or Celebrate Recovery—change your people, places, and things.

A New Start

We relocated to Northern Illinois, and God began to transform us and how we lived every day. We remarried, and this time God became the head of every area of our lives, our marriage, our parenting, our work, our children's schooling, and especially the selection of friends that we would allow to have influence in our lives.

Over the past 14 years, Tony and I have enjoyed sharing what Jesus has done for us and our family. We want to show others what Jesus has to offer. So often when a new believer goes to the altar and asks Jesus into his or her heart, we say, **"Your sins are forgiven, now go and sin no more"** (Author paraphrased John 8:11). What does that even mean or look like? We forget people do not know what this new life is supposed to look like.

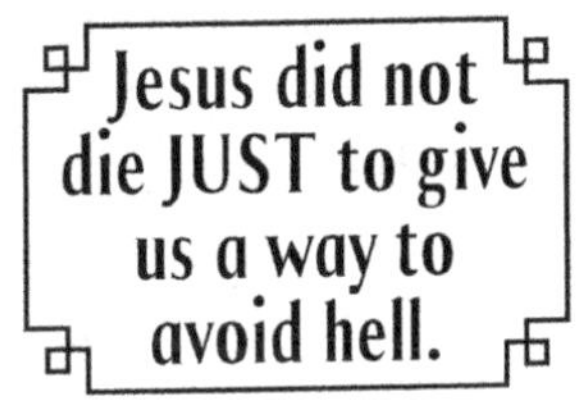

The discipleship process of Celebrate Recovery has a very high success rate. We must show people what works, and it works if you work it. Over the past few years as we have been leading the group, we have had dozens of men and women struggling with porn and sexual issues. Again, it is not a program, a book, or a single preacher that saves. The difference is the blood of Christ and the Word of God applied to everyday living. I want to share several steps we have found that worked in assisting me with continued freedom.

No. 1. Connected to a relationship with Jesus: 15 and 15

Pastor Andy has taught me the necessity of a minimum of 15 and 15 a day. That means, 15 minutes in the Word of God, and 15 minutes in prayer with God. This is the only way you can get and stay connected to Jesus.

When we have a relationship with someone it means we know them. And in order to get to know Jesus, you have to be in His Word. Remember, you cannot obey what you do not know. I find that devotionals are helpful with special verses to read daily. Tony and I have done several devotionals over the years, *Sparkling Gems* by Rick Renner has been one of our favorites as it teaches the Greek meaning behind many of the words we see over and over in the Bible.[1] There are many Bible apps, but I enjoy the YouVersion Bible app, because it lets you see multiple versions at the same time. Reading

---

[1] Rick Renner, *Sparkling Gems From the Greek, Vol. 1* (Fort Bragg, NC: SVS Press, 2003).

through your Bible is important. I started with John because he referred to himself as the disciple Jesus loved. Oftentimes, when we sell ourselves short and settle for a life or relationships that are not God's best for us, it has to do with not believing we are loved. Bottom line: In order to know God, His will for your life, and the good things He wants to do for you and in your life, you MUST read His Word, meditate on His Word, spend time in His Word, and memorize His Word. Even if you only read one verse a day, spend time repeating that verse, looking up different Bible versions that define that verse for a better understanding. Get in the Word!

A fun challenge we did with our kids over the years, was reading the Proverb for the day of the month. Whoever could "guess" which one was my favorite or Dad's favorite first would get a dollar. This season was when I had to give Steven a dollar for snack at school anyway, so this just gave me a way to give it to him while keeping him engaged and in the Word! John shares how even to this day, because of the years we had them read the Proverbs, he can quote more Proverbs than most 25-year olds he knows. And again, don't think we were great, fantastic parents. There were weeks I forgot to hold my kids accountable and check if they read. But, start a habit now! It is never too late to start reading God's Word with your family!

Spend time talking to God. I think a lot of believers underestimate prayer. My husband prayed for me all those years, and I know he intercedes on my behalf countless times. I think about when that pastor's wife gave me the book, *The Power of a Praying Wife,* [2] and how that changed my whole view on my marriage, on parenting, on everything.

Prayer has the ability to unlock faith. Once my pastor preached on dualistic tendencies and how everything is at war in the spiritual realm. Opposites, counterfeits, fleeting happiness—Joyce Meyer often says, "You can have faith or fear, power or pity, but you can't have both."[3] When Tony first got out of prison and we remarried, I told him I was gripped with fear over my niece who used to babysit for me all the time. She was hanging out with a friend's daughter from the drug culture. This young girl was one whom I had seen the drug dealers look at. I shudder even now at the thought. Tony told me every time the Enemy hands me a thought of fear or worry, to unleash a prayer of protection over my niece. I had to speak life over that moment like he did for me while in prison. When I look back at moments I should have had bad outcomes and yet no horrible consequences took place, I know he was intervening on my behalf in the prayer realm. When the Enemy hands me fear, I turn loose a prayer and give God something good to create with my words.

Remember, the key is an ongoing relationship, not a religious checklist of do's and don'ts. To keep

---

[2] Stormie OMartian, *The Power of a Praying Wife* (Eugene, Oregon: Harvest House, 20114).

[3] Joyce Meyer, *Enjoying Everyday Life* (Podcast).

a relationship strong, you have to spend time getting to know the other person. We do that in God's Word, and in prayer.

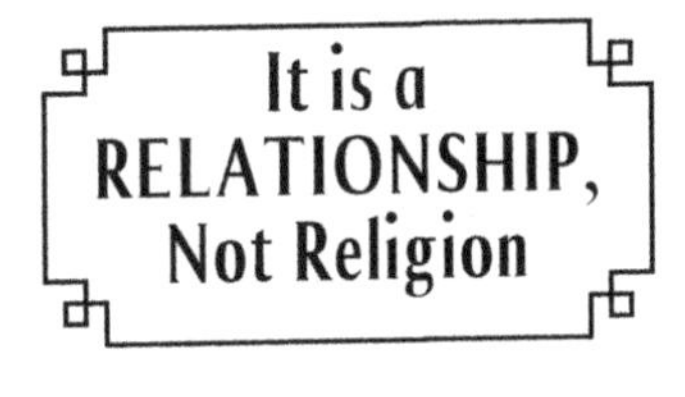

#2 Garbage in Garbage Out, Holy in Holy Out.

My initial book was going to be about the desensitization of our youth through the media. What you watch and hear makes a difference. You cannot watch porn and expect to have a loving relationship with your spouse. You cannot watch violent shows on T.V. if you struggle with rage and anger toward other people or your kids. You are feeding that fleshly monster and keeping hatred stirred up in your heart. You cannot watch people who socially drink and party all the time and stay clean from drugs and alcohol. The same goes for listening to music from the club . . . to constantly play back memories of living it up in your flesh, you are keeping that fire alive. I remember once a guy who worked for us tried to get me to change the station from Christian music to Alicia Keys. The old Nikki loved Alicia Keys. She may have some good songs; however, I told him the reason I would never question my husband being a faithful husband is because I don't listen to songs about how two different girls are fighting over the ownership of a man, or how someone stabbed a tire and keyed a car because someone was cheating, or how doing this and that on the downlow was no big deal. I told him "I don't give the Enemy ammunition to make me question my husband's love for me. Garbage in;

garbage out! I don't have time for that." So, I listen only to Christian music. That may not be your conviction. But if you find you are having a hard time thinking or encouraging positive thoughts, let me challenge you. Like Joyce Meyers says, "Think about what you are thinking about."[4] Whatever you put in is what will come out. I had plenty of women invest in me. All the wise women, the women I would aspire to want to be like, guarded their hearts and eyes.

I listen to books on audio every day. With this comes much access to knowledge, why wouldn't you want to know how other Christians have overcome their struggles? If "**faith comes by hearing, and hearing by the word of God"** (Romans 10:17 NKJV), why would you not want to increase your faith? Also, since I know **"we overcome by the blood of the Lamb and the word of our testimony"** (see Revelation 12:11), I enjoy listening to testimonies. Now I have five or six audio books that I have listened to about overcoming homosexuality, sex, and our youth, the LGTBQ community and their agenda in our schools, all while working on this book. I have already shared about Jackie Hill Perry's book, *Gay Girl, Good God*. In it she makes a reference to dying to her flesh every time she puts on a pair of ladies' underwear. As the dominant one in the relationships, this really registered with me. God created me to be feminine. And now, I see certain things as dying to my flesh.

---

[4] Joyce Meyer, *Enjoying Everyday Life* (Podcast).

Before her book, I never had that revelation—not just about freedom from sex, or homosexuality, but all kinds of freedom.

So garbage in, garbage out refers to all media—T.V. shows and movies, video games, Facebook and Instagram, radio stations and music videos, and books and magazines. Any form of information you can put into your body through the gateways of your eyes or ears is included. We must guard against anything meaningless or harmful, and be sure not to allow it in. We must also be intentional to put in good faith-building, family-friendly media.

#3 Strong Front Row.

I pass this poem out at Celebrate Recovery and to girls often. My sister shared it with me about three years into my new walk with Christ, and around my home with all the kids we talk about the theater and the front row on a regular basis.

Everyone Cannot Be in Your Front Row

Life is a theater so invite your audiences carefully.
Not everyone is holy enough and healthy enough to have a FRONT ROW seat in our lives.

There are some people in your life who need to be loved from a distance.

It is amazing what you can accomplish when you let go, or at least minimize your time with draining, negative, incompatible, not-going-anywhere relationships, friendships, fellowships, and family!

Everyone Cannot Be in Your FRONT ROW.
Observe the relationships around you.
Pay attention: Which ones lift and which ones lean?
Which ones encourage and which ones discourage?
Which ones are on a path of growth uphill
and which ones are just going downhill?
When you leave certain people,
do you feel better or feel worse?
Which ones always have drama
or do not really understand, know, or appreciate you
and the gift that lies within you?

Everyone Cannot Be in Your FRONT ROW.
The more you seek God and the things of God,
the more you seek quality.
The more you seek not just the hand of God,
but the face of God,
the more you seek things honorable.
The more you seek growth,
peace of mind, love, and truth around you,
the easier it will become for you to decide
who gets to sit in the FRONT ROW
and who should be moved to the balcony of your life.

Everyone Cannot Be in Your FRONT ROW.
You cannot change the people around you ...
but you can change the people you are around!
Ask God for wisdom and discernment and choose wisely
the people who sit in the FRONT ROW of your life.
Remember that FRONT ROW seats are for special
and deserving people and those who sit in your
FRONT ROW
should be chosen carefully.
Everyone Cannot Be in Your FRONT ROW.

—Author: Unknown

Do you understand you will become like the five people you spend the most time with? ***Bad company really does corrupt good manners*** (see 1 Corinthians 15:33). ***A prophet receives no honor in his hometown*** (see Luke 4:24). Which to me means ... you cannot go back to the mud pit you just got out of, pointing a finger and trying to rescue others. They will pull you back in. Matthew 7:20 teaches us, *"[So] you will recognize them by their fruit"* (NET). I have had to sit back and watch people's lives to make sure they line up with the words they speak to know if they are healthy enough for me to place in my inner circle. There is nothing wrong with being selective about the people you spend time with. Here are just a few scriptures to back this up.

- ***Listen to counsel and receive instruction, that you may be wise in your latter days*** (Proverbs 19:20 NKJV).
- ***A wise man will hear and increase learning, and a man of understanding will attain wise counsel*** (Proverbs 1:5 NKJV).
- ***The fear of the Lord is the beginning of knowledge; fools despise wisdom and instruction*** (Proverbs 1:7 NKJV).

Who is in your circle of friends?

- ***I am a friend to all who fear You, and to those who keep Your precepts*** (Psalms 119:63 NKJV).

Who are the five people you spend the most time with? Do they fear the Lord and take the Word of God seriously? Even I have to continually reevaluate who I am allowing to be close to me. Yes, I spend a great deal of my time mentoring those who want help. However, I must keep the scales level. Who is pouring into me?

> **In the same way, older women are to be reverent in behavior, not slanderers, not addicted to much wine. They are to teach what is good, so they may encourage the young women to love their husbands and to love their children, to be self-controlled, pure, homemakers, kind, and submissive to their husbands, so that God's message will not be slandered** (Titus 2:3-5 HCSB).

I am extremely intentional about having godly women who challenge me, hold me accountable, love me, pray for and with me, and encourage me in my sphere of influence. I also am intentional about investing in young ladies who appear to be wanting to change their lives. You will know them by their fruit. Their actions will always speak louder than words. I do tend to allow myself to be used and walked on. However, I am getting better at discernment, and I listen to my husband who has my best interests at heart. He is excellent at discerning people.

So, guard your front row.

#4 Church

When the church doors are open, we are there. Let's face it: I didn't just do drugs one day a week, so why then would I give God only one day a week? Hebrews 10:25 says, **"Not abandoning our own meeting together, as is the habit of some people, but encouraging one another; and all the more as you see the day drawing near"** (NASB). *The Passion Translation* reads this way: **"This is not the time to pull away and neglect meeting together, as some**

have formed the habit of doing, because we need each other! In fact, we should come together even more frequently, eager to encourage and urge each other onward as we anticipate that day dawning." Earlier in the book I referred to myself as a "pew sitter," because that is really all I was doing. Now I can see that going to church is the bare minimum a believer is asked to do. Early on in my walk with Jesus, I see how filling our time with church events and ministry was part of my healing and freedom. Seeds from sermons and testimonies, parenting and marriage conferences, Christian concerts, and worship nights were all being sown into my heart. Being in community and having a support network helped me to build lasting friendships. Even though we are all broken (church people sin too), you are not as likely to get yourself in a heap of trouble hanging out with other like-minded believers. For your information, I have walked out of meetings, and had to leave Bible studies where the standards were below what I knew God was calling me to. This is a distinction we have to learn to make, going back to not all people are healthy or holy enough to be around. And if this happens, DON'T GIVE UP. Great churches, events, Christian gatherings, and recovery groups are out there. Sometimes, you just have to go through a few not so great ones to get to the treasure!

Think of it this way: You like to eat more than one time a week. Well, your spirit man needs to be fed more than once a week. Feed your faith and starve your flesh. I had a friend at the last Christian school where I worked, and she referred to me as a "church whore," because we just loved to attend many different churches. Yes, I have a home church, but I learned from Francis Chan that you get what you are expecting. I go into a church expecting God to show up; expecting Him to teach me something; expecting to learn something new. And without fail, God continues to grow me daily.

#5 Give! Give of your time, talents, and your treasure.

Time: When there is an opportunity for us to serve, we give our time. From the nursery in children's church to the concession stand at our boys' school, we invest our time. What you spend your time doing shows where your heart is. Matthew 6:21 says, **"For where your treasure is, there your heart will be also"** (HCSB). About six months ago when they were announcing "Pulse classes," our church's name for Bible study small groups, I made the comment I was so excited to do the marriage Bible study with my husband. My friend turned around and told me, we (Tony and I) were the one couple who did not need that Bible study. But the reason my marriage is as great as it is, is because we invest time in it. We continue to grow closer with each passing year. We love growing together with God. We are intentional about putting our marriage first after our relationship with God. We invest our time.

Talents: We serve, we volunteer, we work, we raise funds. Tony and I have a Helps Ministry. We are hard workers and enjoy working together for the Lord. We have been part of several remodels at our kids' schools, multiple churches, recovery houses, and recently my work where we hold our Celebrate Recovery meetings. We have been part of, or in charge of, auction dinners, garage sales, bake sales, and many other fund raisers to raise money for the Kingdom. If you have special talents that God has given you, then the Kingdom needs them.

The Holy Spirit has made me aware that there will be many people who will stand in judgment of me, thinking that I am writing this book to toot my own horn. But, really, I am writing this book so that when people are sick and tired of being sick and tired, and they want to change their lives but do not know how, they can find hope in my words. Look! My husband and I have been the Celebrate Recovery directors for more than three years now. That does not mean we run up in the bars, or to parties where people may be doing drugs and tell people, "turn or burn." That is ridiculous. We wait for people who want help to come to us. Same thing here. I do not plan to go trying to sell my book and push my advice at the swinger clubs and porn industry trying to upset the applecart. (I should be careful saying what I am not going to do . . . sometimes God sees that as a challenge.) So to the best of my knowledge, we plan to continue to do ministry just like we have for the past 14 years, sharing our story, using our talents!

Treasures: We give back to God. You cannot outgive God. Luke 6:38 says, **"Give, and it will be given to you; a good measure—pressed down, shaken together, and running over—will be poured into your lap. For with the measure you use, it will be**

measured back to you" (HCSB). I remember one Wednesday when our bank account got below a comfortable place, I asked Tony about cutting our tithe check in half. He said, "No way, we would always give to God what is His." We had invested some money with a friend as he remodeled a house, and his home had sold, so he retuned our investment plus some back. We do not put God in a box. He owns and created everything. God continues to bless us in such a way that we love to give and sow money into other ministries. In fact, when Satan tries to get us to reflect on "lack" in some way, I almost enjoy coming back with the comment, "Well, my God owns it all and He will never leave me begging for bread. I know he will provide for all my needs!!" Not just to show Satan, but I know where my help comes from. So, I stir up that spirit of praise and keep the spirit of Thanksgiving in my heart!

Again . . . these are not the magic five steps to sobriety, or purity, or how to go from gay to straight. Jesus and my walk with Him is where my freedom comes from.

This book is to serve as a warning: Sexual sin is increasing, and we must be intentional to **"Come out from among them, and be . . . separate"** (2 Corinthians 6:17 KJV).

Conclusion

In closing, I want to leave you with this. Jesus warns us when teaching about the last days how we should, **"Remember Lot's wife"** (Luke 17:32 KJV). So what do we know about Lot? Genesis 13 (author's paraphrase) says, We know Lot went with his uncle Abram, and they worshiped God together at an altar. God blessed them both so abundantly that as their herders began to quarrel, they had to part ways. And Abram gave Lot first choice. He offered to go to the left or right, it did not matter to him. When Lot looked out over the land, he chose the land well-watered surrounding Sodom. We are told that Lot "pitched his tents" near Sodom, meaning he looked upon the city day and night. Remember, "where you stare, you will steer." We know from the next chapter (Genesis 14) that Lot became a captive, and Abram came to his rescue. And by Chapter 18, we find Abraham pleading with God not to destroy the whole city. He began to bargain with God saying: If You, God, can find 50 righteous, will You spare the city? Abraham continued to bargain and bring down the numbers to 45, then 40 . . . all the way down to 10. Abraham did this to save his nephew, Lot, and Lot's family, because Lot went back to Sodom.

We have all heard the story. After all, the very act of two men being together gets its name from the city of Sodom—the place God destroyed for its wicked acts of homosexuality. Next, two angels go in and Lot protects them from the mob of men who want to have their way with them. Lot even offers up his virgin daughters, (not sure about that one). And they are able to get out of the city just before God destroys it. However, they are warned to run for their lives, and not to look back. In Genesis 19, we are told that Lot's wife looked back and became a pillar of salt *(see v. 26).*

This example shows us how our surroundings affect us. This man went from worshiping at an altar to returning to the city that did despicable things in the eyes of God. What was he thinking? Billy Graham's wife, Ruth, was quoted saying, "If God doesn't punish America, He'll have to apologize to Sodom and Gomorrah." Do you think we get that, when we allow compromise into our churches, and homosexuals into the pulpit?

Jesus warns us in Matthew 24:12: **"Because iniquity (which is sin), shall abound, the love of many shall wax cold"** (KJV). To *wax cold* means, "to grow cold gradually." If you were once on fire for God, just like when a candle is lit, the wax is moldable; but when that candle goes out, the wax begins to harden. This is the way sin creeps into a believer's heart.

It does not happen overnight—it never does. Do you remember "Slow Fade" from Chapter 2? But before you realize it, you could be calling good evil, or evil good. Things that you once had a conviction about, you cannot even recognize as sin anymore. We live in a world where sin is increasing. Our culture tells us things are ok that we know are not. We must stand up, speak out, and protect others. I am convinced that it is the love of God that will help this hurting, broken world. Romans 5:8 tells us, **"But God proves His own love for us in that while we were still sinners, Christ died for us!"** (HCSB). Christ died for all of us, and it is time we start loving the sinner, and hating the sin. I know my moment when God changed my life forever, when I could **"see the kindness and the goodness of God that drew me in, and made me want to repent"** (author's paraphrase, Romans 4:2). There is a new song "Holy Water," and it has a verse about not abusing grace, but how it is the only thing that really makes me want to change. God's unwavering love is what really draws my heart next to His. The only way for you to know God intimately is to spend time with Him. I pray you are in a Bible preaching/teaching church. I pray you will reach out and ask for help. Remember, **"you have not, because you ask not."** James 1:5 tells us that if we ask for wisdom, God will give it generously without finding fault.

Now is the time. The one thing I have observed is that in the past the LGBTQ community has done a much better job educating, recruiting, and discipling (indoctrinating) people into their group than many Christians. I am writing this book with plans to share God's truths. We Christians need to do a better job protecting our children's eyes, training up our families, and discipling other believers.

I have talked with hundreds of likeminded Christians who agree with me. The best thing we have gotten out of "COVID-19" is that the core Christians have become stronger, wiser, and more educated than ever before. The family has been reminded of the importance of the dinner table. The "remnant" is beginning to grow. The sleeping giant has been awakened.

Now is the time. Let's Go!

Bibliography

Anderson, Kirsten. Video. *Faith, Homosexuality, Marriage* (4.7.2015).

Annie E. Casey Foundation. https://www.aecf.org/about/.

Chan, Francis and Lisa. *You and Me Forever: Marriage in Light of Eternity* (San Francisco, CA: Claire Love Publishing, 2014).

Clark, Chap. *Hurt: Inside the World of Today's Teenagers* (Grand Rapids: Baker Academic, 2004).

Coolio, "Gangsta's Paradise." From Music from the Motion Picture Soundtrack: *Dangerous Minds* (Universal City, CA: Soundtracks, Ã1995).

Crowder, Steven. Website: LifeSite News (April 7, 2015).

Department of Justice. Statistics on Abuse.

Dre, Dr. "Housewife." *Hittman and Kurupt Album* (2001, Released in 1999).

Furtick, Steven. *Meant to Be"* Series. YouTube.

Furtick, Steven. *Sun Stand Still: What Happens When You Dare to Ask God for the Impossible* (Colordo Springs, CO. Multnomah Books, 210).

Graham, Billy. "When the Holy Spirit Has Come." *The Holy spirit: Activating God's Power in Your Life* (Waco, Texas: Word Books Publisher, 1978).

Johnson, Ben. Website: LifeSite News (August 13, 2015).

LGBT. *Suicide Stats for Teens*. May 6, 2019.

LifeSite Podcast.

Merriam-Webster's Online Dictionary. Accessed October 17, 2020. *http://www.m-w.com/dictionary*.

Meyer, Joyce. *Battlefield of the Mind: Renew Your Mind Through the Power of God's Word* (New York: Faith Words, 2007).

Meyer, Joyce Ministries. *Enjoying Everyday Life* (Fenton, MO: Joyce Meyer Ministries, Podcast, 2004).

Meyer, Joyce. "Joyce Meyer TV Program."

Omartian, Stormie. *The Power of a Praying Wife* (Eugene, OR: Harvest House, 1997).

Oxford English Dictionary. (n.d.). *http://www.oed.com/view/Entry/156942#eid1211161030*.

Perry, Jackie Hill. *Gay Girl, Good God* (Nashville: B&H Books, 2018).

Renner, Rick. *Sparkling Gems From the Greek*, Vol. 1 (Fort Bragg, NC: SVS Press, 2003).

Rivers, Francine. *Redeeming Love: A Novel* (Colorado Springs, CO. Multnomah Books, 2007).

Site for Screen Time Printed Data.

Shapavalov, Ivan. Website: IMVDB, author, Adam Fairhorn (October 6, 2020). *https://imvdb.com/blog/2014/02/music-video-relapse-all-the-things-she-said-by-t-a-t-u-2003.*

TerKeurst, Lysa. *It's Not Supposed to Be This Way: Finding Unexpected Strength When Disappointments Leave You Shattered* (Nashville: Nelson Books, an imprint of Thomas Nelson, 2018).

Nikole's Dad and Siblings

Nikki

The Old Nikki

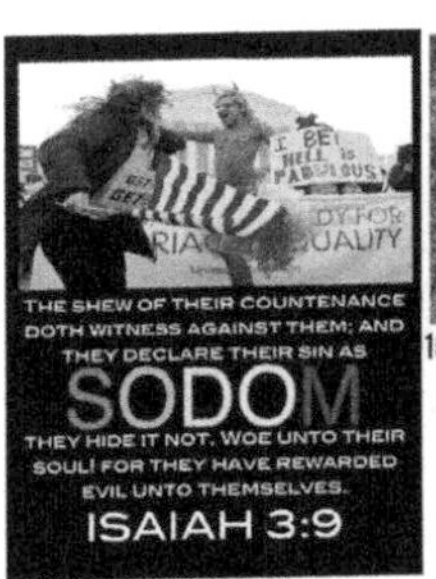

I remember mocking God just like this.

10 YEARS OFF METHAMPHETAMINE TODAY. PRAISE JESUS

LOVE

Tony

This is us.

Our Family

Alexander's LSU Graduation

My dad, mom and siblings

Baby Hazel's Baptism

Dad, my siblings and me

Christian concerts

Tony teaching J.J. strong work ethic

Healing

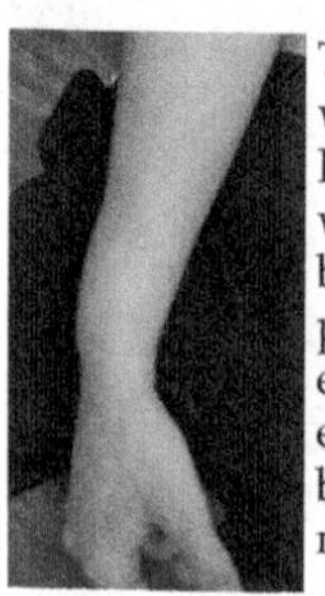

The doctor's were sure Freddie's arm was broken, but many prayed, not even it was not even hurting by the next morning.

Tony urged me to quote healing scriptures over myself to fight against the sickness. It was a week before my son's wedding, and ten years to the day that my mom died. I remember Satan telling me I was going to die just like my mom did (she had that same tube down her nose). The doctors and nurses were telling me I would miss my son's wedding. It was a huge eye opener to the words of our mouths and the direct effect they have on how quickly we get out of the wilderness.

Bible Studies

Youth Conferences

Women's Retreats

Mentors

Celebrate Recovery

Get rooted and planted in a church and start serving.

Walking in Parade

Pastors praying over Freddie as he leaves for Air Force

Family Fall Festival

Delivering Christmas gifts

Working in food bank

Delivering Christmas gifts

Serving in local community outreach and service

Training, certifications, and intentional growth

Speaking life to our kids

Made in the USA
Monee, IL
04 April 2021